COMMUNICATION TECHNOLOGIES AND SOCIETY

Conceptions of Causality
and the Politics
of Technological Intervention

Joanna & Gary Ginter
5840 West Midway Park
Chicago, Illinois 60644

5-18-84

Joanna and Gary Ginter

COMMUNICATION AND INFORMATION SCIENCE

A series of monographs, treatises, and texts
Edited by
MELVIN J. VOIGT
University of California, San Diego

William C. Adams • Television Coverage of the Middle East
William C. Adams • Television Coverage of International Affairs
William C. Adams • Television Coverage of the 1980 Presidential Campaign
Mary B. Cassata and Thomas Skill • Life on Daytime Television
Hewitt D. Crane • The New Social Marketplace
Rhonda J. Crane • The Politics of International Standards
Herbert S. Dordick, Helen G. Bradley, and Burt Nanus • The Emerging
    Network Marketplace
Glen Fisher • American Communication in a Global Society
Oscar H. Gandy, Jr. • Beyond Agenda Setting
John S. Lawrence and Bernard M. Timberg • Fair Use and Free Inquiry
Robert G. Meadow • Politics as Communication
William H. Melody, Liora R. Salter, and Paul Heyer • Culture,
    Communication, and Dependency
Vincent Mosco • Broadcasting in the United States
Vincent Mosco • Pushbutton Fantasies
Kaarle Nordenstreng and Herbert Schiller • National Sovereignty and
    International Communication
Ithiel de Sola Pool • Forecasting the Telephone
Dan Schiller • Telematics and Government
Herbert I. Schiller • Who Knows: Information in the Age of the Fortune 500
Indu B. Singh • Telecommunications in the Year 2000
Jennifer Daryl Slack • Communication Technologies and Society
Dallas W. Smythe • Dependency Road
Janet Wasko • Movies and Money

In Preparation:
Alan Baughcum and Gerald Faulhaber • Telecommunications and Public
    Policy
Gerald Goldhaber, Harry S. Dennis III, Gary M. Richetto and Osmo A. Wiio
    • Information Strategies
Heather Hudson • Telecommunications and Development
Armand Mattelart and Hector Schmucler • Communication and Information
    Technologies
Vincent Mosco • Proceedings from the Eleventh Annual Telecommunications
    Policy Research Conference
Keith R. Stamm • Communication and Community
Sari Thomas • Studies in Communication Volumes 1–2
Tran Van Dinh • Independence, Liberation, Revolution
Georgette Wang and Wimal Dissanayake • Continuity and Change in
    Communication Systems

COMMUNICATION TECHNOLOGIES AND SOCIETY
Conceptions of Causality
and the Politics
of Technological Intervention

Jennifer Daryl Slack

Purdue University

Ablex Publishing Corporation
Norwood, New Jersey 07648

Library of Congress Cataloging in Publication Data

Slack, Jennifer Daryl.
  Communication technologies and society.

  (Communication and information science)
  Bibliography: p.
  Includes index.
  1. Communication—Technological innovations.
2. Communication—Social aspects. I. Title. II. Series.
P96.T42S5 1983   001.51   83-15693
ISBN 0-89391-124-0

Printed in the United States of America.

ABLEX Publishing Corporation
355 Chestnut Street
Norwood, New Jersey 07648

For those readers among you
who can appreciate its strengths
and forgive its weaknesses.

Contents

Foreword

Lawrence Grossberg

Communication scholars suffer from a common interactional affliction: a defensiveness that results from having repeatedly been asked to explain, "what exactly is it that you do?" or "what exactly is the field of communications?" Communication is the closest the intellectual world has at the moment to a Hollywood star: simultaneously loved and resented, it has a real mystique, both because it apparently cuts to the heart of our contemporary existence and because it increasingly appropriates the intellectual space of other disciplines. But unlike other "magical" disciplines in the past—for example, political economy in the nineteenth century—communications did not choose to be an imperialist power; it had its position in the academic world thrust upon it, or, more accurately, created by other discourses and the media. Ironically of course, these are the very stuff that communications studies. The reasons for this odd position are unclear and certainly complex and include the mislabelled "communications revolution" and the emergence of communication at the heart of many twentieth century philosophical anthropologies.

The discomfort that this situation produces for communications scholars is evident in the textual strategies that many of them adopt. Recognizing the impropriety of the global claims of communication, they constantly seek either to circumscribe the discipline or to justify its claims by substituting philosophical anthropology for communication theory. Further, recognizing the lines that connect their theoretical investigations with issues of political intervention, they (re-)produce the political neutrality of research and deny its inevitable political underpinnings. More recently, having been called upon to speak in the political arena, they accept the invitation as a concerned citizen rather than as a communications scholar, and thus refuse to draw the political implications of their research. Even on the "left", the political intervention is often so mechanically reproduced that the research seems an unnecessary detour. The analysis is often oversimplified; the result is, predictably, humane outrage at the capitalist and technological degradation of existence. There is, however, a new generation of critical communications researchers who are unwilling to hide these dilemmas in the aporias of their textual strategies. They seek ways to integrate communication into a larger theoretical framework, stubbornly maintaining the local character of communication and rejecting its global pretensions. They seek ways to connect theoretical (and epistemological) investigations with political interventions, refusing to exclude or isolate either moment.

Dr. Slack's *Communications Technologies and Society* is an excellent and elegant example of the work of this new generation. She is concerned with the critique of technology: that is, the interpretation and evaluation of the place, functions, and effects of any particular technology in its social and political context. After all, actual political intervention into the future development and implementation of communications technology must at least implicitly assume that it understands the forms in which the relations between technology and society emerge. Slack's assumption is that technology is a form of human practice rather than some objective and external agent which either acts entirely on its own or is the simple pawn of human manipulation. If technology emerges, is defined, shaped, and implemented, and has its effects always as one mode of practice among others, then the question of technological critique becomes one of the "overdetermination" of social practices. In Slack's terms, what lies at the root of our inability to understand our technological environment and to intervene productively in the shaping of its future is an inadequate theory of causality. The contemporary modes of critique and intervention—"technology assessment," "alternative technology," and "luddism"—all fail to recognize the complex processes by which technology shapes and is shaped by the world of social practices. Using Althusser, Slack demonstrates that the practical failure of such positions is inseparable from their theoretically inadequate assumptions about technology (as an historically determined and determining mode of practice) and about social causation. Althusser's model of overdetermination provides Slack with an alternative way of approaching and structuring the complex processes by which a particular technological practice comes to exist and have material effects.

In its simplest terms, the theory of overdetermination says that any mode of practice is determined by its relationship to all of the other modes of practice in the social space, but these other modes are already determined by other practices, including those that they determine. There are no agents of causality that can be isolated and simply manipulated. It is a causality whose existence is the very structuration of its effects. The problem that seems to stare one in the face, however, is what one can possibly say about such a system. It is here that Slack has done such a service, for she has admirably demonstrated that the complexity, the inability, to ever completely isolate a simple set of causal or expressive relations need not mean that one cannot make useful and insightful interventions, both hermeneutically and politically. In her penultimate chapter, she begins to reconstruct historically a piece of the complex system (an historically existing social formation) to produce some of the puzzle: namely to examine the relationship between a particular set of legal practices (patent law) and the practices of technological innovation (more than simply invention or origin, the crucial question is the processes by which particular technologies have been incorporated into or excluded from the social formation, and the ways in which the particular form of that exclusion or incorporation have been determined). Her conclusion offers us an understanding (albeit necessarily partial) of the relation between these two sets of practices, and draws out the implications of this relation for current issues in communications technology. The result is a specific, and, I would imagine, *controversial* proposal for a political intervention: the refusal to grant patent protection to computer software. This might seem to contradict our normal assumption that patents protect individual rights. Slack's argument, however, is that a careful examination of the effects of patents reveals that they have operated in a very different way, one which in the notion of "intellectual property" protects the economic and corporate appropriation of technological innovation. The particular intervention is not proposed as a radical undermining of contemporary structures of power (although its repercussions are interesting to consider), nor as an apocalyptic opening of a utopian future. It is a concrete proposal, based on a careful analysis of the contradictions in the institution itself, which would alter at least the way in which the technological environment is determined.

It is a modest proposal, caught between Slack's theoretical and political practices. The concreteness of her analysis belies the remaining moments of her utopianism. It is sufficient, to give credence to her prescription, that, as Foucault might say, she would give voice to those who have been silenced. There is, beyond the verbal and conceptual strategies of the argument, an epistemological and political practice that is both acknowledged and deferred. For example, by using Althusser's theory of the "levels" of the social formation to identify modes of practices, Slack's practice limits the strategic possibilities of the theory of overdetermination. Slack's text occasionally reinscribes the very boundaries it has already transgressed but then, what text does not? I want therefore to intervene into the reading of this text, to draw new lines connecting it to slightly different theoretical and political strategies.

Slack connects us with Lenin's call for a truth which is always concrete. The result is a critical practice which inscribes itself into the context as an intervention, both theoretical and political. But in so doing, it inscribes as well the limits of its claims, for it is a theoretical practice condemned to the concrete. It is not that critical theory is not necessary, but rather that the practice of critical theorizing is an act of invocation and bricolage; of producing the objective historical context from a point that can never be outside. A theory of overdetermination is a practice of "fictioning the real." It is the production of a truth from the ruins scattered about the environment, the facts impinging upon our practices and desires, impediments to and signposts of our utopian fantasies, and structures of power. One builds the context from the bottom up, subtracting anything but the specific factual pieces of the puzzle. Of course, there is no end to the puzzle; one can always add more pieces. That is the humility of theory, but it is a humility which refuses the relativistic denial, the positivistic reduction, and the transcendental utopian justification of its truth. We speak of facts, and our speaking is itself one of the facts, an intervention that is a part of the context because it is both produced by and effective within the context. There can be no escaping that we talk from a position within the context (a position both determined and politically active) and no reason to deny the truth of our position. For truth is measured merely by its effects; it is a question of power and therefore, of both macro- and micro-politics. Critical theory is, then, not a set of assumptions but of slogans, a toolbox for the production of truth: be more concrete! draw more lines! subtract more identities and correspondences!

We can see this in Slack's silence on the concept of communication, her refusal to constitute a category of the 'communicative'. There is a growing body of discourse—emerging from both philosophical reflection and research programmes—revolving around the constitutive role of communication in human life. Yet it is another case of the elusive quark: the more we assume that communication is the soul of our humanity, the less we are able to say about this transcendental term. It recedes from our conceptualizations as well as from our attempts to locate it empirically. All we can ever identify are communicative practices, always plural, always existing as material events in our historical and social environment. While the discourse of overdetermination ruptures the structures of power that organize our experiences, the discourse of communication reconvenes those structures, reterritorializes our existence in the concrete facticity of events and desires. It draws the lines between various practices from a point apparently above their facticity and effectivity. And thus it occludes its own political functions. Three discursive strategies operate here: first, communication is given a transcendental status; second, a widely diverse set of practices is subordinated to an imposed identity; and third, a particular reduction of the multiple and contradictory subjectivities of human existence is carried out. The communicative subject is produced as an the imperial subject. Questions of power are reduced to those of communicative equality, freedom of access, and the free flow of information (as if these are ever actual events). Thus, a critical theory of communication faces a unique dilemma since its very discourse reproduces some of the very relations of power that it seeks to identify. The only solution is, apparently, to transgress not only those lines which circumscribe the concept of communication, but also those which differentiate its modes of existence: e.g. as institutions, it is studied by political economy; as texts, it is studied by cultural studies. But as practice, it is a concrete struggle to invoke without naming.

This struggle is political as well as theoretical. It is a political strategy that refuses to begin with notions of an experienced crisis (e.g. alienation, lack of control, degradation) and refuses to end with appeals to revolution (technological or political) and utopia. It starts and ends with practices, their conditions of possibility, and their effectivities. It remains local: at best is has available a set of tools to be used, adapted or discarded. While it invokes our sense of self and community, it dismantles them into temporary and regional alliances. It is not coincidental that this political practice is not only emerging on the left, but is already an active strategy of the so-called "new right." This is, however, not sufficient reason to abandon the strategy for the practices of two positions having effectively opposed vectors. Both acknowledge their own existence within relations of power. For the "new right", the strategy involves ideological interventions which, in the name of transcendental ethical principles, reinscribe boundaries of political and affective authority. For the left, however, the strategy implicates practices which "ferret out the fascism that is ingrained in our behavior", (Michel Foucault's "Preface" to Gilles Deleuze and Felix Guattari, *Anti-Oedipus: Capitalism and Schizophoenia*, New York, 1977). Such practices constantly struggle against their own claim to power, deterritorializing the realities they produce: the very inscription of boundaries is the source of the possibilities of totalitarianism implicit in any structure of power, in any claim to authority.

These speculations about epistemological and political practice are stimulated by Dr. Slack's book because the text speaks of the need to find new ways in which to understand and intervene in our environment. The urgency of the book, despite its humility, is the anonymous and inescapable urgency that results from new objective practices demanding new strategies of response. Dr. Slack has made an important contribution, both theoretically and politically, to this struggle.

Preface

This book challenges the ways we think about communication technologies. Too often scholars have written about communication technologies without a critical eye toward the ways in which they explicitly (though more often implicitly) characterize the relationship between communication technologies and society. Consequently, scholars frequently locate technologies and society in positions that are theoretically inconsistent, contradictory, or indefensible.

Communication Technologies and Society sorts out and critiques both the explicit and implicit conceptions of the relationship between communication technologies and society. In particular, it isolates conceptions of the causal relationship between communication technologies and society as a principal source of obfuscation and misdirection. Technology does not *cause* society. Nor does society *cause* technology. Rather, technology is developed and used *in* society, in the complex interplay of social forces that are at the same time both cause and effect.

We are living in a time when scrutinizing our theoretical understanding of the role of communication technologies in society ought to be paramount, for the ways we think about technologies are intimately related to what we do about them. And if there ever was a time when we ought to tred thoughtfully and cautiously in technological matters it is now—as information technologies assume not only a national but a global significance that promises to surpass the significance of industrial technologies.

The dominant force behind the preparation of *Communication Tech-*

nologies and Society has been a search for an articulate, theoretically compelling, and practically powerful model for understanding and affecting the ways in which social structures and practices are related to the development and use of communication technologies. My search began after reading N. R. Danielian's account in *A.T. & T.* (1939) of the way in which the patent pools of the 1920's divvied up control of the technological world as though it were exclusively corporate property to be manipulated merely to please the interests of capital. I had been quite naive about political economy and was shocked to discover the ways in which the machinations of the corporate world, armed with patent law, could effect the development of our means of communication. I owe considerable thanks to Thomas Guback for guiding me through the literature on the political economy of communications, for dispelling the naiveté, and for providing the conceptual tools for researching the political economic levels of communicative processes and practices. Furthermore, the honesty and integrity with which Tom conducts his own research provides a model I can only strive to match.

Political economy, however, can not alone account for the apparent complexities of the relationship I seek to articulate. In particular, political economy does not address adequately the role of ideology in the development and use of communication technologies. It also does not account for the ideological nature of the inadequate practices of presumably well-intended scholars utilizing what seem to be terribly flawed conceptions of the relationship between communication technologies and society. But one cannot simply "add on" ideology to the study of political economy. To understand the role of ideology, the nature of the totality within which politics, economics, *and* ideology operate must be rethought. For guiding me through the complexities of that rethinking, through much of the world of the philosophy of communications, I thank Lawrence Grossberg. Larry has been considerably influential on the final shape of *Communication Technologies and Society.* His enthusiasm and support for my interest in enriching the concrete study of communications with the theoretical insights of, in particular, cultural studies and structuralism, have encouraged my search for meaning irrespective of traditional disciplinary boundaries.

Colleagues and friends have provided the intellectual and emotional environment that have made *Communication Technologies and Society* both possible and pleasurable. Three individuals are particularly special to me; they are a part of me. Fred Fejes offered loving support from beginning to end, making life and work joyous. Eileen Meehan talked, shared, cared, read, reread, critiqued and performed that oft underrated task of keeping the spare copy in case of fire! Martin Allor helped separate the seriousness from the silliness in my attempts at understanding, particularly in struggling to apply structural causality to the development of patent law.

In addition I thank Kenan Jarboe for his assistance on the chapter on Technology Assessment; Vincent Mosco for helpful suggestions for revising the entire manuscript; Scott Murto who, as the first person who read the manuscript almost solely because he wanted to understand what was in it, insisted on revisions for the sake of clarity; C. Jan Swearingen and Gary Witherspoon for valuing scholarship in an otherwise sad time at the University of Michigan, where Jan and I lived through the dismantling of the Department of Humanities; and my family (Pam, Joe, Linda, Su and Ted) for believing in me.

Various institutions and the people who work within them also receive my gratitude. At the University of Illinois, I thank the Institute of Communications Research for a supurb and somewhat unorthodox graduate education; the University Archives and archivists for making the files of Joseph Tykociner available; and the fine Communications Library for unparalleled service. At the University of Michigan, I thank the Rackham School of Graduate Studies for a grant to continue research in the Joseph Tykociner files.

As this project grew—from individual research papers, to a dissertation, and finally to this book—I began to reach out to a broader audience, for I have become increasingly convinced that all communication scholars as well as all inhabitants of this era touted as the "information age" could benefit greatly from understanding explicitly that the ways we think about the relationship between communication technologies and society have philosophical and theoretical underpinnings as well as implications for acting in that relationship. I am grateful to Ablex Publishing Corporation, particularly editor Melvin J. Voigt, for providing the institutional support for sharing my convictions.

Jennifer Daryl Slack
Purdue University

chapter one

The Context for Technological Criticism and Intervention

With technological change in communication proceeding at an ever accelerating rate, particularly with respect to information technologies, developing a basis for sound technological criticism and active intervention is crucial. Criticism must be firmly grounded in an adequate understanding of the relationship of technologies to society and to change. Intervention—that is, entering into that relationship to hinder or modify it—must be grounded in a sound theoretical understanding of the relationship if it is to be effective. To develop sound technological practices—practices involving both criticism and intervention—we must challenge as guides for such practice, our dependence on a fascination with technology as well as our dependence on the unexamined attribution of tremendous causal powers to technology. In short, we must learn to be critical; but being critical means something far more complex than fault finding.

The confusion regarding the use of the term "critical" is difficult to set straight, given that it is deeply rooted in the nature of what it means to do criticism. Qualitatively different activities are often all labelled as "criticism." The common use of the term "critical" is simply that of fault finding. Yet any judgment passed on the merits or "demerits" of a technology must be firmly grounded in an understanding of the historical relationship of that technology with society. Technology does not spring forth in full regalia, like Minerva from the head of Zeus, armed to do battle for good or evil. Rather, technology is called into existence by a particular set of historical circumstances that shape and define the tech-

1

nology. We must understand that set of historical circumstances if we are to comprehend the effective relationship between technology and society. Such comprehension constitutes a fuller sense of the term "critical." Thus, while some analyses of communication technologies may find fault and suggest strategies for intervention, they may not be particularly critical. When analysis is based on an inadequate understanding of the nature of the relationship between technologies and social structure, intervention based on that analysis is likely to be inadequate, for it is likely to misunderstand seriously the nature of the effective relationship between the technologies and the social structures within which they arise.

This book analyzes and critiques the predominant forms of contemporary technological intervention, as well as the conceptions of the relationship between technology and society on which they are based. All too often, the so-called critiques of technology offer little illumination vis-à-vis the relationship between technology and society. As a consequence, they cannot lay a firm foundation for the establishment of informed, thoughtful, technological intervention. The goal of this book is not, however, merely to understand the inadequacies of contemporary technological practices. Rather, the ultimate goal is to use the analysis of their inadequacies to develop a more profound theoretical understanding of the effective relationship between communication technologies and society—an understanding that can form the basis for sound technological criticism and intervention.

Out of the desire to control technological growth and the effects—both beneficial and deleterious—of particular technologies, three approaches have assumed paramount importance: (1) Technology Assessment, (2) Alternative Technology, and (3) Luddism. *Technology Assessment* is an approach that was developed originally to address government interest in the enhancement of the positive effects of technology and the mitigation of its negative effects. It has become essentially a method for studying the effects of technologies on society, with special emphasis on secondary and unintended impacts. *Alternative Technology* is a term that loosely describes the orientation of various groups whose approach to technology criticism and intervention is anticorporate and procommunity. The concerns of these groups are much the same as the concerns of the counterculture movement. *Luddism* takes its name from a group of workers in nineteenth century England that rioted and destroyed machines to protest the social injustices that the machines represented. The term has come to refer to anyone who destroys machines or who believes that certain machines are unacceptable because they can produce only negative effects.

Interestingly, the most recently formulated approach, Technology

Assessment, is also the most rigorous and well focused. Yet, its ability to critique the relationship between communication technologies and society is the most circumscribed. Technology Assessment is also bound quite closely to the decision-making processes of business and government. On the opposite side of the scale, Luddism is probably one of the oldest and most complex responses to the development of modern technology. While Luddism can provide researchers with tools for a broader survey of the relationship between technologies and society, it is least serviceable for the interests of business and government. Alternative Technology lies somewhere in between these two. The approach is better focused than that of Luddism, though not as focused as Technology Assessment. Alternative Technology does not serve business and government as conspicuously or consciously as Technology Assessment, but it does serve to the extent that Luddism does not.

These three approaches provide an interesting corpus of contrasting attitudes toward technology, spanning extremes in political, economic, and philosophic practice. In Section I, I analyze these three influential "critical" perspectives in order to assess the degree to which they really are critical of technology, in the sense of being based on an understanding of the relationship of technologies to social structure. In particular, I assess their underlying attitudes toward technology and technological growth. Finally, I evaluate their consequent strengths and limitations as tools for guiding appropriate technological intervention.

Underlying all responses to communication technologies—indeed the building blocks of any pronouncement about the effective relationship between technologies and society—are notions about causality. In short, how we think about technologies, as well as what we "do" with and about them, is integrally related to our sense of the causal relationships between technology and society. To better understand the deficiencies and limitations of Technology Assessment, Alternative Technology, and Luddism, Section II explores the deficiencies of the conceptions of causality that form the foundations of these perspectives. Three conceptions of causality are considered: simple, symptomatic, and expressive causality. Because there is no simple one-to-one correspondence between the perspectives and the conceptions of causality, these conceptions are first explored somewhat autonomously. Then the roles played by the various conceptions of causality in Technology Assessment, Alternative Technology, and Luddism are discussed explicitly.

Significantly, the models of causality developed in Section II can be applied broadly. Their immense explanatory power extends far beyond the limited use to which I have put them here—as the philosophical underpinnings of Technology Assessment, Alternative Technology, and Luddism. Few positions taken by anyone on technological criticism and intervention do not manifest the characteristics of one of these causal models.

This study is undertaken with dual purpose: one is to understand better the deficiencies of contemporary technological criticism and intervention. The other is to begin to evolve a more productive framework in which to study the effective relationship between technologies and social structure for the purpose of formulating guidelines for technological intervention. Consequently, Chapter 7 suggests adopting an alternative conception of causality—structural causality, which can overcome the deficiencies of the conceptions of causality that underlie inadequate technological criticism and intervention.

The test of any theoretical formulation is its ability to generate compelling explanations that provide productive tools for interacting with empirical reality. Thus, Chapter 8 analyzes a principal aspect of the effective relationship between communication technologies and social structure, utilizing the structural model of causality developed in Chapter 7. This analysis explores the relationship between the structure of patent law and processes of the invention and innovation of communication technologies. As the analysis illustrates, a structural causal model leads one to a very different kind of criticism of the relationship between technology and society, for it considers the effectivity of the complex historical circumstances that give rise to technology and within which technology is an effective force. Intervention based on this model can now be directed toward particular effective aspects of the complex relationship between technology and society.

Finally, Chapter 9 explores some of the possibilities for, along with the consequences of, taking the approach developed in this book beyond the case of patent law and the invention and innovation of communication technologies. The particular suggestion is that the notion of the technological revolution is based on an inadequate model of causality. Furthermore, by utilizing a model of structural causality, the notion of a technological revolution in communication can be seen as an ideological construct that propels a characteristic kind of technological development. Chapter 9 concludes with criticisms of the structural causal approach developed in the book, pointing to particular areas where additional investigation might enhance its efficacy. This is, after all, just a beginning.

SOME THOUGHTS ON THE USE OF THE TERM "TECHNOLOGY"

A few words of explanation. Focusing on the technologies of communication rather than on technologies in general is warranted—if not called for—given the unique role often ascribed to communication technologies. Yet scholars who study the technologies of communication draw heavily on arguments and concepts developed within the study of the relationship between society and technology in general. Therefore, in deference to necessity as well as to usefulness, I will often draw on the more generalized literature on technology and society in order to facilitate understanding the relationship between communication technologies and society.

In addition, it is incumbent on anyone writing a treatise on technology to define what is meant by the term. Doing so is not an easy task, for a plethora of definitions must be considered. Nevertheless, the task of definition is of critical importance, for the way in which we define technology, or conceive of it, influences our attitudes toward it, our understanding of it, and our prescriptions for changing it. A definition of technology is, ultimately, a way of seeing. Since one of the goals of this book is to engender a new way of seeing technology, it is imperative to challenge old definitions while exploring and cultivating new ones.

The term "technology" has undergone a radical expansion and a corresponding dilution of meaning. In past centuries, according to the *Oxford English Dictionary,* "technology" referred to "the scientific study of the practical or industrial arts" or the "practical arts collectively." In the twentieth century, the term has become increasingly problematic. "Technology" is now a widely used term with meanings that range from machines, tools, and devices to organizations, systems, and techniques. In response to the changing usage, *Webster's Third New International Dictionary* defines the word as "the totality of the means employed by a people to provide itself with the objects of material culture."

Currently, in the scholarship on technology and society, debate over the definition of technology occupies a position of considerable importance. The debate often revolves around distinctions between tools and machines, devices and knowledge, applied science and technology, and the like.[1] Two threads appear consistently in definitions of technology: technology as a device or physical structure and technology as the social organization, means, or realization of the principles of scientific arts. The former theme focuses on the device, which might be a structure, tool, machine, or naturally occuring object. The latter focuses on social, economic, and political structures or values that may be personified by the device or that may implement the device. Sometimes social organization is the device.

The current vogue in writing about technology is to combine the two threads in defining technology. Lewis Mumford's definition, which does so, has become, for many, the preferred definition. In *Technics and Civilization,* Mumford (1963) uses the term "the machine" to refer to both machines, by which he means both specific objects and the entire technological complex. This complex embraces "the knowledge and skills and arts derived from industry or implicated in the new technics, and will include various forms of tool, instrument, apparatus and utility as well as machines proper" (p.62). Some contemporary commentators on technology drop explicit reference to the tool, instrument, apparatus, utility, or machine in deference to a definition emphasizing social organization. Langdon Winner (1977b), in "On Criticizing Technology," is satisfied to use Mumford's definition of "technics" as a working definition of technology. Quoting from Mumford's *Art and Technics*, "technology" or "technics" is, for Winner, "that part of human activity wherein, by an energetic organization of the process of work, man controls and directs the forces of nature for his own purposes" (p. 356).

There are advantages in adding the dimension of social organization to the definition of technology. There are even advantages in limiting the definition of technology to the dimension of social organization. By embedding technology in social organization and practice, we acknowledge that technology is not an autonomous, isolated force, unconnected to the rest of society. The new definitions acknowledge an interrelatedness among social structure, values, and the machines and structures themselves. The new definitions also acknowledge that, in their interrelatedness, devices organize social practice, and they are thus integral parts of social organization and practice. It is difficult to capture this sense of interrelatedness if we envision mere "things" as the objects of study.

We would expect, then, that the expanded definitions of technology would permit, if not encourage, a conception of technology as intergral to social structure and practice. And to some extent, they do. Yet they also permit, if not encourage, a corresponding dilution of meaning. This dilution of meaning actually discourages critical analysis of the complex relationships between technologies and social structure and practice. This apparent contradiction occurs because the new definitions tend to collapse technologies and social organization into a single homogeneous conception of technology and society that is based on a simple reflective hypothesis. An uncomplicated correspondence is often assumed between social organization and devices. Thus, to use an extreme example, Jacques Ellul (1964) maintains that our world is what it is because the machine made it that way. Technique, which integrates the machine into society, "has fashioned an omnivorous world which obeys its own laws and which has renounced all tradition" (p. 14). "Machines," "technology," "technique" and "society" are thus reduced to virtually synonomous terms. Each term becomes a mere reflection of the others. Another example is Mumford's oft cited discussion of the relationship between the clock and social structures and values. The clock, according to Mumford (1963, p. 13), was an "almost inevitable product" of the monastic life. Regularity and accuracy pervade them both.

The simple reflective hypothesis, as illustrated by such examples, usually reduces the natures of both social organization and the machine to a single dynamic. Thus, for Ellul, the modern world directly reflects the mechanical nature of the machine; the machine defines society. For Mumford, the clock directly reflects the social organization of monastic and, eventually, all human life; the clock symbolizes the activity of humanity. When utilizing a simple reflective hypothesis, researchers search for the unidimensional correspondences. Lack of correspondence or contradictory dynamics are of little or no consequence. If any importance is assigned to them, they are usually considered to be aberrations rather than data. The reflective hypothesis thus dilutes or disposes of the examination of complicated contradictory relationships between the technologies and social organization.

As this book is concerned primarily with exploring a new way of characterizing the relationship between social organization and technology, it is absolutely essential to begin by questioning the nature of that relationship. The study must begin by admitting the possibilities of both correspondence and contradiction. The reasons for rejecting the formulations of technology that collapse social organization and technology into any single dynamic are therefore obvious. Consequently, the term "technology" means machines and structures, not social organization.[2] As opposed to "technology," the phrase "technical system" will be used when referring to the social organization involved in the implementation of a technology. By utilizing the conception of a technical system, I acknowledge the integral role of social organization in the implementation of technology. I am not, however, reducing or limiting the nature of the technology to a reflection of a singular dynamic of social organization. Neither am I reducing social organization to a reflection of a singular dynamic of technology. Drawing these analytical distinctions enables one to analyze the relationship between technologies and society, while admitting a full range of possible contradictions and correspondences.

The raison d'être of this work is to find more accurate and productive ways to explore and to define the relationships between communication technologies and society, in order to lay a foundation for technological intervention. As a consequence, questions of definition will be raised as pertinent evidence provides clues to what it means to talk about communication technologies and how to prescribe meaningful and effective technological intervention.

FOOTNOTES

[1] For a wide range of positions on the intrinsic nature of technology that both directly and indirectly address the issue of definitions at this level, see Mitcham and Mackey (1972).
[2] For a discussion of the distinction between structures and machines, see Billington (1974).

section
one

Contemporary Critiques
of the Relationship
Between Communication
Technologies
and Society

chapter two

Technology Assessment

Technology Assessment refers specifically to an approach developed to assist government in assessing the positive and negative effects of technologies. The purpose of this assessment is to aid the government in generating rational technological policies—policies that will enhance the desirable effects of technologies and mitigate the undesirable ones. More generally, Technology Assessment has come to signify a method for studying the effects of technologies, with an emphasis on secondary and unintended effects. In both these senses, Technology Assessment has become an influential tool for talking about the relationship between communication technologies and society. Consequently, it has become an influential basis for generating technological policy in communications. To evaluate Technology Assessment as a potential critical tool, we must understand the relationship between Technology Assessment as a Congressional capacity and the approach as a more generalized method. It is similarly important to explore the relationship between Technology Assessment as a theoretical formulation and as a practice.

THE HISTORY OF TECHNOLOGY ASSESSMENT

To assess, according to *Webster's,* is "to analyze critically and judge definitively the nature, significance, status, or merit of" something. In this sense, to assess technology is not really to do anything particularly new. Individuals and institutions regularly assess the merits of technologies.

For example, institutions assess technologies when they choose whether or not to develop them. Consumers assess technologies when they choose whether or not to buy them. Conscious and deliberate assessment of technology has been conducted by government for some time, but historically it has been executed primarily after the fact, that is, after serious damage has occurred or after there has been a public outcry. For example, only after a tremendous outcry by concerned parents, teachers, and social critics did the government become involved in assessing the effects of television on children.

The process of assessing the merit, significance, or status of a technology may be either conscious and deliberate or subconscious. Criteria for measuring these attributes vary, depending on the pecularities of the assessor, the purpose for which the technology is being assessed, and the socioeconomic/political context in which the assessment takes place. Examples of the breadth of measures by which relative merit, significance, or status might be gauged are use-value; the extension, expansion, or solidification of market control; the attainment of status; and the service to another's interests (such as that of society, another individual, or an institution).

The measurement of merit and demerit can involve the assessment of a technology from three temporal viewpoints: historic, contemporary, or futuristic. The last gains preeminence in assessing for the purpose of deciding to purchase, exploit, develop, or regulate a technology. In this situation, the potential merits and demerits are projected, as well as perhaps the relative merits of various alternatives. Judgment is then passed, and a basis for action laid that is expected to produce the greatest benefit, in accordance with the aims in the particular case.

Decisions in real life, however, are rarely as rational as this process might suggest. Real decisions are often based on convenience, ignorance, spite, or coercion. Besides, a decision that may appear to be rational to one observer may appear to be irrational to another. Decisions can appear to be—and may in fact be—haphazard, devoid of any rationale, or even in opposition to the best interests of both the decision makers and those affected by the decisions.

As the concern over possible deleterious and irreversible effects of technology intensified in the late 1960s, the "mood" of many in Washington turned progressively toward a cautious skepticism of unrestrained technological development. The growing fear was that such development could have considerable impact on the survival of our nation and perhaps even of the planet. In this mood of cautious skepticism—armed with the knowledge that technological decisions are all too often based purely on self-interest or on some other less desirable criteria—a movement began. This movement was interested in developing a rigorous, institutionalized, Congressional Technology Assessment capability. The motivations of the individuals and groups involved in this movement were varied (Berg, 1981, 477–478). Some participants, who were apparently interested in suppressing or controlling the development of "advanced" technologies, were not very successful in defining the scope of Technology Assessment. Instead, the "good government reformers" or the "rational policy advocates" won the day. This decidedly protechnology group was interested primarily in enhancing technological development. The minimization of undesirable side effects was one way to ensure enhanced development.

The credit for giving the imprimatur to both the terminology and to the current meaningfulness of Technology Assessment is probably best ascribed to the efforts of Emilio Q. Daddario (Teich, 1977, 223). In 1967, while chairman of the Subcommittee on Science, Research, and Development of the House Committee on Science and Astronautics, Connecticut Congressman Daddario introduced a bill calling on the federal government to establish a Technology Assessment Board "to provide a method for identifying, assessing, publicizing, and dealing with the implications and effects of applied research and technology" (U.S. Congress, 1967). Daddario (1968) believed quite strongly that "technological changes have become so extreme and occur so rapidly that it is incumbent upon us to reverse the process" (p. 1044). In addition to the hope that a Technology Assessment Board might be able to "anticipate and minimize the unwanted side effects which so often accompany innovation," Daddario was hopeful that such a board might be able to streamline or rationalize technical development, particularly given the high cost of modern research and development. "A Technology Assessment capability for Congress," Daddario asserted, "will enable us to deploy the finite scientific and engineering resources of money, facilities and skilled manpower to take fullest advantage of the gains offered to society" (p. 1046).

Daddario's bill was not passed in the late 1960s. By the early 1970s, however, numerous federal agencies claimed to be conducting Technology Assessment-type studies and the National Science Foundation had begun funding Technology Assessment projects. (Porter, 1980, 34–47). The Office of Technology Assessment (OTA) was finally created by Congress in 1972, pursuant to the Technology Assessment Act of 1972. The OTA received funding in November 1973 and began operating in January 1974. Daddario became its first director and remained in that position until May 18, 1977. The basic mandate of the OTA was to "provide Congressional committees with assessments or studies which identify the range of probable consequences, social as well as physical, of policy alternatives affecting the uses of technology" (U.S. Congress,

1975, p. 4). Six priority areas, as designated by the OTA's Congressional Board, were adopted: oceans, transportation, energy, materials, food, and health (U.S. Congress, 1975, 15). Later these areas were subsumed by three major divisions: energy, materials, and global security; health and life sciences; and science, information, and transportation (U.S. Congress, 1979, 3).

Until 1978, most assessments were conducted in response to specific requests from Congressional committee chairpersons or ranking minority members. Beginning in 1978, an effort was made to assess technologies based on an internally drafted "priority list of issues of critical concern to the United States and the world." The final decision to assess a technology depended on the possibility that it might have significant impact, that assessment might provide foresight, that there was Congressional interest in the issue, and that the OTA was capable of performing the task (U.S. Congress, 1979, p. 4).

Communication technologies were not initially a priority area of interest to the OTA. Only a few studies of communication technologies were conducted before 1978, the first being an assessment of the value of broadband communication systems in rural areas (U.S. Congress, 1976). In 1978, the OTA established the Telecommunications and Information Systems Group, as a response to the rapid advance and subsequent importance of new communication technologies (U.S. Congress, 1979, 55–56). Furthermore, the OTA had been asked by several Congressional committees to assess aspects of the changing communications scene. Two assessment projects specifically concerned with communication technologies were initiated in 1978. The first was to assess the societal impacts of national information systems; the second was to assess the impact of new telecommunication technologies such as satellites and fiber optics (U.S. Congress, 1979, 56–57). The first of these studies was released in 1981 (U.S. Congress, 1981); the second was never completed. However, numerous other relevant studies have been completed and/or promised since 1981 (see Slack, forthcoming).

THE THEORY AND METHODS OF TECHNOLOGY ASSESSMENT

Trying to separate the theory of Technology Assessment from its practice is a tempting idea, for there is considerable debate, discussion, and argument about what Technology Assessment ought to do or could do, as opposed to what it does do.[1] Yet despite some differences between what Technology Assessment could or should do and what it does do, both the theory and practice of assessment seem to be grounded in some crucial assumptions that are of considerable consequence for Technology Assessment's ability to interpret the relationship between technology and society and to intervene in that relationship. The next two sections focus first on the *theory* and *methods* of Technology Assessment, in order to address its theoretical and methodological shortcomings, and then on the *practice* of Technology Assessment, in order to illuminate the ways in which the theoretical weaknesses invade the practice.

Technology Assessment is not really about assessing technologies in the original sense of "to assess." Recall the dictionary definition of assess (one that Daddario used frequently): "to analyze critically and judge definitively the nature, significance, status, and merit of." Now compare this definition of assess with the definition of Technology Assessment that has been very widely accepted as an appropriate definition of institutionalized assessment: "the systematic study of the effects on society that may occur when a technology is introduced, extended, or modified, with special emphasis on the impacts that are unintended, indirect, and delayed" (Coates, 1974, p. 77). There are many distinctions between these two definitions, but two are particularly significant, vis-à-vis the theory and methods of Technology Assessment. The first is a shift from assessing a whole technology to the study of its effects. What of technology *as* an effect? Second, the study of effects is further limited by the emphasis on unintended, indirect, and delayed effects. What of the intended, direct, and immediate effects? An examination of these emphases alone renders Technology Assessment questionable as an adequate critical tool for analyzing the relationship between communication technologies and society and for intervention in that relationship.

Technology Assessment focuses on the impacts or effects of technologies. Analysis usually begins with the identification of impact areas: first macro areas (such as the economy) and then micro areas (such as the GNP or employment). Researchers then identify the chain of specific impacts of a technology in these macro and micro areas. Thus, for example, the computer might be seen as causing fewer jobs for clerks, which causes unemployment, which causes retraining, which causes employment. Different studies will bound (that is, limit the length of) these causal chains depending on a number of such factors as the purpose of the study, the methodology employed, or the concern for limiting the extension of the chain to the point where the researchers feel certain that they are still talking about the effects of the technology.

As this example illustrates, Technology Assessment does not take into account the context within which the technology appears initially. Technology Assessment does not consider the question of technology as both cause and effect. So, for example, the cause of unemployment can be traced only to the computer. It cannot be traced to the particular

political, economic, and ideological configuration within which computers arise. If the computer was searched for, invented, and innovated
primarily as an efficient method of decreasing labor costs and enhancing
efficiency, the "cause" of unemployment would be every bit as much (if
not more) attributable to the ideology of efficiency, economic strategies,
contradictions between labor and capital, and the conjunctures between
them. Appropriate intervention would have to be based on an assessment of the totality of those relationships of which the technology was a
part. Only then would assessment and intervention really be based on
the nature, significance, status, and merit of the technology.

Confounding the problems of conceiving of the relationship between technologies and society as merely one in which technologies have
effects, Technology Assessment tends to limit the consideration of effects to those that are unintended, indirect, and delayed. As a consequence, it is unlikely that assessment would ever acknowledge or assess
the primary motivations for which a technology might have been invented and innovated. Technology Assessment does tend to affirm—if
only tacitly—the primary functions of technologies as well as the intended motivations for their implementation. Technology Assessment thus
tends to be not only a highly conservative activity, but one that is assert-
ively so. Technology Assessment professes to "assess," when what it really does is offer legitimation. To understand this dynamic, consider the
way in which Technology Assessment equates technological development with progress.

THE POLITICS OF TECHNOLOGY ASSESSMENT: TECHNOLOGICAL GROWTH AND PROGRESS

In September 1967, the Subcommittee on Science, Research, and Development, under Daddario's chairmanship, sponsored a Seminar on
Technology Assessment with the intent of beginning an exploration of
the issues involved in Technology Assessment as embraced by the bill
submitted earlier. At the request of the House of Representatives, both
the National Academy of Sciences and the National Academy of Engineering undertook to study Technology Assessment and to submit
reports of their findings. In particular, the two august academies were to
explore the following aspects of assessment: "what it means to various
groups, how it occurs today, how it is related to the behavior of individuals and organizations, how its quality might be improved and its
influence enhanced" (U.S. Congress, 1969b, p. 7). The reports submitted by the National Academy of Sciences (NAS) (U.S. Congress, 1969b)
and the National Academy of Engineering (NAE) (U.S. Congress,

1969a), in addition to an article by Daddario (1968) published in the *George Washington Law Review* in 1968, best characterize the intent and spirit of Technology Assessment. Despite slight differences between the reports, all fundamentally ascribe to the same brand of faith in technological progress. Although these documents formed the basis for Technology Assessment as a Congressional capacity, they also largely determined what it means to practice Technology Assessment as a general method. These three documents will elucidate this faith in technological progress as fundamentally a political commitment.

The impetus for the genesis of Technology Assessment emerges as twofold. Technology Assessment is at once a response to the negative consequences of technological development due to unplanned, anarchic freedom, as well as a response to the desire to fully exploit technologies—in the guise of progress. Such exploitation requires the minimization of possible public dissent and the maximization of possible positive input. This twofold impulse was expressed in Daddario's desire for a Technology Assessment Board to streamline technical development, and it was similarly expressed in the "Summary of Findings" of the NAE report: "Unless dependable means are developed to identify, study, and forecast the varying impacts that these technological developments might have on sectors of our society, the nation will be subjected to increasing stress in a time of social turbulence and will not benefit fully from technological opportunities" (U.S. Congress, 1969a, p. 3).

To monitor undesirable social effects while fully exploiting potentials, the NAS argued that a rigorous standard for assessment was required. The report recognized that assessment of technological prospects based primarily on self-interest had become quite widespread in both the private and public sectors. One problem with such self-interested analysis, the NAS maintained, was that it:

may ignore important implications of particular choices for sectors of society other than those represented in the initial decisions. In their pursuit of benefits for themselves or for the particular public they serve, those who make the relevant decisions may fail to exploit technological opportunities that, from a broader perspective, might clearly deserve exploitation. Likewise, as they seek to minimize costs to themselves, the same decision-makers may pursue technological paths that, again from a broader perspective, ought to be redirected so as to reduce undesirable consequences for others. A wide variety of what economists call external costs and benefits thus falls "between the stools of innumerable individual decisions to develop individual technologies for individual purposes without explicit attention to what all these decisions add up to for society as a whole and for people as human beings" (U.S. Congress, 1969b, pp. 9–10).

The goal of Technology Assessment is to provide information that

———

will allow policy makers to correct deficiencies in the uses of technologies. Indeed, the NAS claimed that the object of their study was not technology *per se,* but human behavior and institutions. Their goal was *"not to conceive ways to curb or restrain or otherwise 'fix' technology but rather to conceive ways to discover and repair the deficiencies in the processes and institutions by which society puts the tools of science and technology to work"* (U.S. Congress, 1969b, p. 15). Technology Assessment, as essentially a service providing information for policy makers, asks the kinds of questions that speak directly to the concerns of policy makers.

While Technology Assessment enables one to generate limited criticism and analysis of the uses of particular technologies, the approach is still firmly committed to the credo that technology is essentially synonomous with progress. Nowhere is this more explicit than in the NAS report, where humans are depicted as "committed to a highly technological culture." Although there are "technologies whose effects we sometimes deplore," these same technologies are responsible for liberating us. These same technologies "are themselves largely responsible for the fact that we both can and do consider the effects of decisions and policies on a much larger part of the human population than ever before." Advances in technological development have enabled us to "anticipate the secondary and tertiary consequences of contemplated technological developments and to select those technological paths best suited to the achievement of broad combinations of objectives." Technological development, in giving us more options from which to choose, has bestowed on us a superior ability to choose. The NAS report grounds its approach to Technology Assessment in "the conviction that the advances of technology have yielded and still yield benefits that, on the whole, vastly outweigh all the injuries they have caused and continue to cause" (U.S. Congress, 1969b, pp. 10–11).

The potential for adequate technological criticism is seriously circumscribed by the assertion that assessment must not become a threat to technological progress. Daddario (1968) maintained that assessment must emphasize not the dangers of proposed technological changes but rather their potential for good. The NAS even suggested that the "burden of uncertainty" due to imperfect knowledge must not continue to be placed on those who develop new technologies and new uses for technologies (U.S. Congress, 1969b, 33–39). We must be willing to take chances and to experiment, for, as Daddario stated, it is "the boldness to try something different, . . . [that] . . . has been responsible for a great portion of our material welfare and strength among nations; it has set our country somewhat apart from other countries of similar culture" (p. 1047). Technology Assessment is thus firmly committed to an almost simpleminded equation of technological development and some notion of social progress. Indeed, the commitment is moderated somewhat, however, in that it is tempered by the realization that some undesirable effects of technology need to be considered to insure such progress. The challenge of Technology Assessment, according to the NAS, is "*to discipline technological progress in order to make the most of this vast new opportunity*" (U.S. Congress, 1969b, p. 12).

THE PRACTICE OF ASSESSING COMMUNICATION TECHNOLOGIES

The theoretical and methodological weaknesses of Technology Assessment, as discussed above, seriously limit its ability to form the basis for sound criticism of communication technologies. Analyzing a few studies in some depth discloses the seriousness of these limitations.

The first study examined is the OTA's earliest and most ambitious assessment of a communication technology, completed in April 1976: *The Feasibility and Value of Broadband Communications in Rural Areas: A Preliminary Evaluation* (U.S. Congress, 1976). In this report, prepared originally for the Senate Committee on Agriculture and Forestry, the OTA raises two sets of questions, both of which fundamentally address the economic feasibility and value of rural broadband communications. Existing broadband systems are defined, for purposes of the study, as systems consisting of one, or combinations of, the following technologies: coaxial cable, translators, ground- or satellite-based microwave relays, and fiber optics. The crucial potential impact of these technologies is depicted as overcoming problems of communication in an economically feasible way in areas of low population density and geographic isolation. Broadband systems, the staff asserts, can "substitute communications for travel in the delivery of public and commercial services" (p. vii). By public services they mean nonentertainment programming and services relating to education, medicine, government, and law enforcement. By commercial services, they mean burglary and fire detection, news programming, stock and commodities prices, automatic meter reading, pay TV, and data transmission.

The first question addressed is, "can such systems be economically feasible in outlying rural areas and, if so, what would be their worth?" (p. vii). The second set of questions is designed more to assess the economic ramifications of the systems rather than the economic feasibility of the systems themselves. "Can broadband systems contribute to the economic development of these regions? How might widespread adoption affect the balance between rural and urban areas? Might they increase the attractiveness of rural areas as places in which to live?" (p. vii). The underlying expectation expressed in the latter set of questions is based on the hope that communications media might facilitate the reversal of the exodus from rural to urban areas. Such a reversal would, they assert, help the country achieve more balanced growth.

The study as a whole is motivated by the concern over the failure of federally supported experiments that set out to deliver nonentertainment services to rural areas over various media, particularly cable television. Cable extension had not been economically feasible in rural areas due to the paucity of subscriber fees per mile of cable. The OTA hoped to make extension economically feasible by authorizing charges for nonentertainment channels and by allowing cable companies to collect revenues from public service and commercial use. So, under the banners of "equity for the rural people" and "rural community development," (p. I–1) the OTA staff explored the ways in which the constraints on the development of broadband communication systems to the rural community could be overcome in such a way to benefit the system owners.

One major roadblock to economically feasible broadband service was regulatory restriction, particularly as imposed by Federal Communication Commission (FCC) regulations, which are discussed in some detail. One particularly troublesome restriction was the regulation that required that certain rural nonentertainment public service channels should be made available free of charge. The concern over this regulation illustrates the study's predominantly economic concern: "although the FCC has sought to encourage development of nonentertainment uses with free channels, the regulations may have had the opposite effect and made it impossible for rural areas to afford either broadband systems or new services" (p. I–12).

The length and breadth of policy alternatives considered in this report are severely limited by the questions that the OTA staff sets out to answer. The only alternatives considered are (1) to maintain the status quo, (2) to fund some additional demonstration projects, and (3) to institute a Federal mechanism to facilitate implementation on a broad basis of the kind of broadband communication system in rural areas that was proposed and explored from the onset of the study.

In the analysis of the pros and cons of each proposed alternative, the desirability of broadband system development to rural areas is simply taken as fact, as is private ownership of the systems. The reason given for the possible maintainance of the status quo is that telecommunications might "eventually come to rural areas without specific Federal assistance" anyway (p. IV–91). Considerations against maintaining the status quo essentially add up to the fact that the status quo cannot guarantee system development and, in fact, will probably insure that development will not occur.

Conducting demonstration projects is seen as desirable, in that further and more specific information could be made available regarding economic feasibility and cost-effectiveness of broadband system development. On the opposing side, demonstration projects take time. Given that the several case study programs discussed earlier in the report suggest that widespread service to rural areas might be economically feasible, further delay necessitated by additional demonstration projects would, the report maintains, only unnecessarily delay services to rural areas.

The entire report is essentially about the positive impacts of implementation of the broadband system. The negative considerations, really just reservations, all involve details of the mechanisms of implementation. For example, the staff recognizes the need to assure the development of program content and computer software. They also feel that, without the proper encouragement to develop uniquely tailored systems and without sufficient imagination as to their use, the proposed services would probably not succeed.

As this analysis demonstrates, the kinds of answers suggested by *The Feasibility and Value of Broadband Communications in Rural Areas* are heavily implicated in the questions asked initially. The disclaimer, presented at the beginning of the report, states that "the study does not resolve these questions but instead describes an approach for seeking out the answers" (p. xi). The assessment is nevertheless firmly grounded in an overall commitment to, and uncritical acceptance of, the nature and role of the technology. The staff suggests that to complete the assessment further studies must be conducted, but these studies would be nothing more than embellishments of the original. No substantially new questions would be addressed. They suggest, for example, that a committee examine "constraints to wider application of broadband communications in rural areas," or that they consider "the possible need for, and best form of, Federal involvement in rural broadband applications in the system demonstration phase as well as in subsequent programs" (p. IV–98).

The study is concerned primarily with finding ways to render broadband communication to rural areas economically feasible, which means, of course, finding ways to assure that the venture will be sufficiently profitable for the private communication companies that would provide the services. The report tacitly accepts, if not outright approves of, the position that the postulated needed services for rural areas cannot be rendered unless the venture is profitable for the communication companies. There is no critical analysis of the needs of rural areas. There is no critical challenge to the preeminence of profitability over those needs. The assessment of the technology, along with the valuation of its nature, significance, status, or merit, turns on its ability to adapt to the requirements of the capitalist economic system.

This study does not address the problem of the relationship between the communication technology and society in any comprehensive way. Communication technologies are tools with which social problems can be solved, but the technologies bear no relationship to those social problems, other than as tools to solve them. The study is a complete affirmation of technology as a force for the betterment of our society and the reparation of society's ills. The government need only insure proper safeguards to avoid failure of the project. Failure, in this case, is the ultimate negative consequence.

The tendency toward the uncritical equation of technological growth with progress is not unique to the OTA, as pointed out by a study sponsored by the National Science Foundation and the Cogar Foundation and conducted at Cornell University by Carl Hershey and Elizabeth Sachter (1976). "Acquiring Baseline Data on Potential Uses of New Communication Technologies" has a twofold purpose. One is to address "the problem of anticipating, in a systematic and disciplined manner, patterns of use of technologies currently in the development stage" (p. 52). The study is thus intended to be, in part, methodological in character. The second intention is to use these methods to assess, if only in a preliminary way, a particular technology: cellular systems of mobile communications. A cellular system is one in which a large area is divided into smaller cells, each of which is covered by a low-power transmitter/receiver. These low-power transmitter/receivers are then connected to a central computing and switching facility by means of lines or high-frequency electromagnetic links. This arrangement allows for broad coverage of communication with mobile units. As a unit moves from one cell to another, communication is monitored through a different cell as determined by the central computing and switching facility.

Hershey and Sachter draw the questions regarding the impact of cellular systems quite narrowly.

Why do organizations and private citizens presently use mobile communication devices? What are the advantages and disadvantages of these mobile technologies? What factors would increase or decrease the attractiveness of the new cellular system for present users of competitive mobile technologies, as well as for persons not using these technologies? What is the magnitude of the potential demand for advanced mobile communications? What are some of the more important likely organizational impacts of such use, e.g., on work activity patterns, on speed and effectiveness of service to clients and customers, and on organizational structure? (p. 53).

Clearly, taken as a whole, these questions guide the analysis to consider who the potential market is for cellular systems and how the technology might best be adapted to accommodate it.

———

Hershey and Sachter measure positive and negative impacts of cellular systems, using a combination of fieldwork and survey research. In
determining which impacts of the technology are desirable to current
and potential users, the terms of measurement are drawn even more
narrowly than the original questions suggest. The study relies on the
users' definitions of positive effects of the technology to characterize, in
a general way, the positive impacts of the technology. As a consequence,
the positive impacts are measured in terms of the technology's ability to
increase productivity, to help the users accomplish their tasks in a more
effective and efficient manner, and to centralize technical advice and
control. Similarly, undesirable impacts of the technology are defined by
potential users, who identify such aspects as a lack of privacy and the
superfluity of the technology.

Hershey and Sachter consider that having the users themselves
identify the relevant impacts is a unique contribution to the methods of
Technology Assessment. Such a method, however, defines the parameters within which technological impacts are analyzed even more narrowly. Furthermore, it seems particularly—and very seriously—limiting
to define positive impacts as those aspects of a technology that a user
deems as useful without critically evaluating those uses. An assessment
of this sort is thus far less critical than even the earlier formulations of
Technology Assessment. The reliance on evaluation by users renders
this study not much more than the self-interested assessment of technologies that Technology Assessment professed to overcome.

Finally, apart from the problems and limitations of assessing the
impacts of cellular system mobile communication, Hershey and Sachter
identify another area of impact that occupies a prominent position in
their assessment. In the two concluding sections of the study, Hershey
and Sachter determine who, given the positive and negative impacts as
perceived by potential users, will in fact be a potential user. The study
climaxes with this determination. The initial questions asked of the data
render the definition of users a cardinal concern. Those who will use the
technology, and to what end, essentially delimit the positive or desirable
impacts; those who will *not* adopt the technology and their reasons essentially delimit the negative or undesirable impacts. Again, just as in the
OTA's broadband communication study, the successful and perhaps
rationalized adoption of the technology is the underlying driving force
behind the assessment.

Not all assessments of communication technologies define the impacts of a technology as narrowly as does the study by Hershey and
Sachter. Some studies cast their nets wider and consider a broader range
of impacts. Most still suffer, however, from the propensity to accept
uncritically the primary function of the technology and equate develop-

ment of the technology with progress. A good example of such a study is Edward M. Dickson and Raymond Bowers' (1974) interesting and inquisitive preliminary assessment, *The Video Telephone.*

Dickson and Bowers cast their net much more broadly than do most Technology Assessments. This unusually thoughtful study explores the ways in which the video telephone might have an impact on areas of socioeconomic life as diverse as the nature of human communication, the structure of organizations, energy utilization, educational and medical services, services for the deaf, the development of complementary technologies such as data transmission, and the effect on the international balance of payments. In patent conformity with the prevailing practice of Technology Assessment, however, the study frames the issues in such a way that the critical evaluation of primary functions and impacts of the technology—as well as its relationship to the socioeconomic structure—is precluded. Such a limitation is not surprising, given that the purpose of the study is to form a basis for policy making that will enhance the likelihood that the technology will be developed, its primary function instituted, and its secondary undesirable effects mitigated. From the beginning of the study, the authors affirm this position when they state that "technology assessment seeks to outline some of the policy options that could maximize the likelihood of beneficial consequences and minimize the likelihood of detrimental consequences" (p. 1).

The study delineates effects—both beneficial and detrimental—but employs critical skills only where those effects are secondary or tertiary. For example, in a discussion of the impact of the video telephone on the structure and location of organizations, Dickson and Bowers assert that the technology is capable of reinforcing the tendencies for organizations to become physically decentralized while remaining linked via computer. They also mention that, while the video telephone may reinforce physical decentralization, it may foster less self-sufficiency, which may in turn increase interdependence and centralization. They do not comprehensively assess the nationwide economic, political, or cultural impacts of this tendency toward apparent decentralization with its corresponding tendency toward centralization of power and authority. They do not, for example, explore the nature of those impacts on the decentralization of the central business districts, an impact brought about and further encouraged by a wide variety of causes, some of which they mention, and one of which is the video telephone. They merely mention that decentralization may "upset many of the current policies and plans to rejuvenate central cities" (p. 121). Presumably, these centralizing/ decentralizing technologies, like the computer and the video telephone, would be employed if companies felt that they would improve their productivity. But the researchers do not explore the consequences of

companies utilizing these technologies ever in search of expanding prof-
its and increased productivity.

Instead of focusing a critical eye on some of these primary aspects of
the video telephone, Dickson and Bowers become taken with the secondary consequences of the technology on the structure and location of
organizations. Productivity within the workplace is a crucial concern. For
example, they analyze the effects that the video telephone might have on
patterns of work. They cite two examples where secretarial services operated more efficiently using the video telephone, thereby increasing the
quality and quantity of work performed. In contrast with this apparent
positive impact, the study points to the fact that workers may be forced
to relocate as a result of continued decentralization. Yet the economic,
political, and cultural consequences of relocation remain unassessed.

The authors reveal their indisputable zeal for the technology in,
ironically, a brief assessment of the undesirable impacts of the video
telephone on face-to-face communication. In short, they suggest that the
decentralization of organizations could render face-to-face communication harder to come by. While the authors call for more research, they
imply quite strongly that we must be willing to accept the new technology
on its own terms and not measure it against older conceptions of desirable communication. Quoting Alex Reid, they recommend bearing in
mind that, "If telecommunications is treated as a simulation of face-to-
face contact it is by definition a second best alternative. In fact telecommunications systems have considerable potential advantages over face-
to-face contact, advantages which will not be exploited if such systems
are treated as inferior substitutes for the real thing" (p. 122). Here the
authors uncritically accept the primary functions and impacts of the
technology. The consideration of "side-effects," or in this case the possible denegration of face-to-face contact, is not even examined in its own
terms. Rather it is strongly suggested that it should be evaluated as a
side-effect to be dealt with only to the degree that is absolutely necessary.
It is subordinated to the primary and, of course, positive effects of
implementation of the technology.

In practice, as all the studies discussed illustrate, the problem of
undesirable effects is obviously subordinated to the primary goal of
successful implementation of the technology. Furthermore, evidence
hints that undesirable effects are—at least in part—defined by political
and economic power. If persons or groups in positions of power object
to the impact of a particular technology, then the impact will likely be
defined as undesirable. Thus, for example, as David Dickson (1974, 58)
points out, an assessment procedure led expert evidence in 1969 to
recommend to the Roskill Commission in England, a commission which
was to determine the location of London's third airport, that it was less

desirable for aircraft to fly over middle-class neighborhoods than over lower-class neighborhoods. The damage to property values would be less in lower-class neighborhoods.

As is the tendency in all Technology Assessment, Dickson and Bowers ignore all "irrelevant" undesirable effects in favor of a strong commitment to implementation of the technology. In this case, the commitment is so strong that the study is, by the authors' own admission, a kind of prophecy. The analysis of impacts presumes that the video telephone will be made available. It further presumes to know specifically what the video telephone of the future will look like and what the relevant institutional and regulatory structures will be like as well. In presuming to know the future, the analysis then leaves little room for the evaluation or critique of alternative scenarios. This study, like Technology Assessment in general, limits the scope of analysis so severely that it is unable to critically assess the relationship between the technology and society in anything other than the most superficial, protechnology manner.

Any researcher, of course, must limit the scope of research. Answering all the questions about any technology in one study, or even in a myriad of studies, is impossible. Yet also absolutely essential is understanding the ways in which any study or research tradition limits the potential for using its formulations as a critical tool to measure and change reality. Technology Assessment is severely limited by an unquestionably uncritical and untenable bias toward technological growth and development. In the case of Technology Assessment, this observation is particularly important to make, precisely because it professes to provide objective, unbiased criticism of technology. Also, this "objective" criticism is used primarily in the policy arena.

It must be noted that the authors of most Technology Assessments are, to some degree, aware of their limitations. Most researchers assert that their assessments are either preliminary or tentative—always pending further information. This qualification implies a recognition that such studies can never be complete, or that no one can ever fully and accurately predict all of the consequences of a technological development. In some cases, researchers are willing to acknowledge the limitations of the study that result from personal bias. Dickson and Bowers (1974, p. 4) acknowledge their personal bias explicitly when they state that, "No single technology assessment can be considered final because of the absence of complete data, uncertainty about the methodology, limitations of the human imagination to foresee all possible interconnections, and, above all, the inability of humans to avoid bias resulting from their personal values. Indeed, personal values can distort the structuring of the assessment itself." The sociological nature of the personal bias, which applies to most researchers engaged in Technology Assessment, favors the equation of technological growth and progress. As a strong supporter of Technology Assessment observes, "technology assessment (TA) has become the province primarily of engineers and economists. As a result TA is somewhat more positive in its stance towards technology, especially new technology" (Brooks, 1979, pp. 466–467).

Of far greater consequence than personal or sociological bias, however, is the bias that is built into the theory and practice of Technology Assessment to begin with—the bias toward asking policy-oriented questions in a way that reaffirms the faith in technology as a tool to solve any and all social problems. This faith insures that Technology Assessment can neither adequately assess the relationship between communication technologies and society nor provide a basis for sound intervention in that relationship. If it could, it would no longer be Technology Assessment.

TECHNOLOGY ASSESSMENT
AND THE IDEOLOGY OF INDUSTRIALIZATION

In the policy arena, Technology Assessment is used as a legitimizing tool, and the questions that Technology Assessment has been called upon to answer have tended to be those that affirm the expansion of technological development in service of increasing productivity. As pointed out by David Dickson (1974, 57–58), Technology Assessment suffers from what he calls the "ideology of industrialization," that is, the belief that the primary function of technological innovation is to maximize efficient industrial production. The main concern of the study of broadband communication to rural areas, for example, was to find a way to make such a broadband system economically feasible, that is, profitable for the communication companies capable of delivering the service.

This faith in the continual advance of technology in service of the ideology of industrialization is certainly not limited to Technology Assessment. Nor for that matter is it limited to the advocates of capitalism. Many Marxists have praised, relatively uncritically, the development of western technology and encouraged the adoption of western technology by socialist countries. V. I. Lenin is well known for encouraging the adoption and adaptation of Frederick W. Taylor's methods of scientific management. Lenin stated in 1918 that the progress achieved in the formulation of scientific management,

like all capitalist progress, is a combination of the refined brutality of bourgeois exploitation and a number of the greatest scientific achievements in the field of analysing mechanical motions during work, the elimination of superfluous and awkward motions, the elaboration of correct methods of work, the introduction of the best system of accounting and control, etc. The Soviet Republic must at all costs adopt all that is valuable in the achivements of science and technology in this field. The possibility of building socialism depends exactly upon our success in combining the Soviet power and the Soviet organisations of administration with the up-to-date achievements of capitalism. We must organise in Russia the study and teaching of the Taylor system and systematically try it out and adapt it to our ends (quoted in Braverman, 1974, p. 12).

It may be unfair to characterize Lenin, based on just this statement, as eager to impose scientific management on Soviet workers. The characterization might, however, be entirely justified, particularly considering that Lenin, in *State and Revolution,* distinctly uses the model of capitalist productivity as a paradigm for productivity within a socialist or communist government (Mendel, 1961, 177–183). While "From each according to his ability, to each according to his needs," may characterize the degree of participation of individual workers, the nature of the work performed remains essentially the same. Lenin writes: "it is quite possible, after the overthrow of capitalists and the bureaucrats, to proceed immediately, overnight, to replace them in the *control* of production and distribution, in the work of *keeping account* of labor and products by the armed workers, by the whole of the armed population" (Lenin, 1917/1961, p. 181). But the model of productivity remains unchallenged, as does the nature of the products being produced. Lenin does little more than decry the *control* of production by capitalists. He assumes that the same technologies used in much the same way (that is, to enhance productivity) by the Soviets is desirable. If capitalists control the technology, then the technology is alienating; but if the dictatorship of the proletariat controls the technology, then it is liberating. By so reducing the relationship between technology and society to a question only of control and accounting, the technology itself escapes analysis and criticism, as does the more complicated relationship between technology and progress. The position advanced by Lenin, then, is almost a mirror image of Technology Assessment. The ideology of industrialization is still the dominant dynamic, reflected in both positions; only the masters served have changed.

CONCLUSION

Technology Assessment has serious limitations as a tool for critiquing the relationship between technology and society. Stemming from the theoretical and methodological formulations of Technology Assessment, these limitations are evident in the practice of assessing particular communication technologies. These limitations can be explained, in part, in terms of Technology Assessment's roots as a Congressional capacity. Even more important, the limitations of Technology Assessment can be understood in terms of its broader commitment to the ideology of industrialization and to equating technological growth with social progress.

If our goal is to intervene in the relationship between technology and society, grounding that intervention in the best possible understanding of that relationship, why would we want to limit ourselves to tools that close off so many crucial aspects of that relationship? Shouldn't we be willing to admit the possibility that technological development is not necessarily synonomous with social progress? Shouldn't our methods of analysis allow us to probe beneath the superficial questions concerning economic feasibility, potential markets, curbing public dissent, and the like? Why would we want to limit ourselves to using methods that have been designed largely to streamline unchallenged technological growth? Alternative Technology and Luddism, the approaches discussed in the following chapters, raise exactly these questions. Both approaches are committed to intervening in the relationship between technology and society, armed with answers to the substantive questions that lie beneath the surface of those asked by Technology Assessment.

FOOTNOTES

[1] For a discussion of the range of debate within Technology Assessment, see Boroush, Chen and Christakis (1980, 350–393).

chapter three

Alternative Technology

Unfortunately, Alternative Technology cannot be described in the same systematic way as Technology Assessment. Alternative Technology is not, strictly speaking, an approach or a set of methods. It is best characterized as a movement—and a broad movement at that—that was spawned by some of the same fears of deleterious and irreversible effects of technology that gave birth to Technology Assessment. Yet it is different in that it identifies the problem somewhere in the conjuncture between technology and corporate interests. Thus, to the extent that the movement can be said to be unified, it is unified by a shared sense of alienation from corporate America and its technology.

This chapter presents an analysis of the commitments of the Alternative Technology movement via an analysis of the movement's relationship to the counterculture movement. The particular configuration of the commitments of the Alternative Technology movement seriously limit its potential for providing a critical understanding of the relationship between communication technologies and society. Interventions based on the commitments of the movement are shown to be not only inadequate but often contradictory to their original intentions.

Sadly, in the Alternative Technology movement's conception of the relationship between technology and society, there is a fascination for technology and technological progress. This fascination is then coupled with the notion—similar to Lenin's, discussed in the previous chapter—that technology can be made to serve a just (read, "anticorporate") society merely by altering the uses to which the technology is put. Ironically,

30

this union of the commitment to technological progress and the belief in technology's malleability renders the interventions of the movement particularly vulnerable to exploitation by just those corporate structures that its disciples despise. Consequently, Alternative Technology has almost as much to offer corporate America as does Technology Assessment.

ALTERNATIVE TECHNOLOGY AND THE COUNTERCULTURE

Alternative Technology is closely allied with the counterculture movement, which became so visible in the late 1960s. Like that movement, the Alternative Technology movement can claim a mélange for a membership. David Dickson (1974, 38) has suggested a number of approaches that can be subsumed under the general rubric of Alternative Technology: soft technology, radical technology, low-impact technology, intermediate technology, people's technology, and liberatory technology. Appropriate technology can also be added to this list. The ends for which these groups work may be as varied as their names suggest. For example, they may be seeking to minimize environmental devastation (by far the largest and most visible group), to liberate mankind from the rhythms of the modern industrial machine, or to develop and utilize technologies that are complementary to the group's particular brand of ideal society.

Despite this variety, the movement seems to be held together by the belief that technology needs to be tamed and that technologies are tools to be developed and employed only in the service of well thought-out social and environmental goals and values. In the words of Ivan Illich (1973, pp. xii–xiii), a proponent of alternative technologies who has achieved the stature of prophet among many alternative technologists, the goal is to develop a society "*of responsibly limited tools,*" a society "*in which modern technologies serve politically interrelated individuals rather than managers.*"

The counterculture has always emphasized an individualist solution to the political, economic, and environmental transgressions that the members deplore, an emphasis that has become even more pronounced since the 1960s. Theodore Roszak (1978), famed popularizer of the counterculture movement, begins his book, *Person/Planet,* with the question, "What ever became of the counterculture?" (p. xxi). He answers with the assertion that the counterculture is alive and well—even thriving. The culture, he maintains, is only less visible because of the intensification of the members' quest for personal growth, spiritual fulfillment, and meaningful interpersonal communication. This search for identity has been accompanied by a move away from visible, political opposition. *Person/Planet* exudes the movement's obsession with the self; the book is in fact dedicated to the task of sketching and elevating the movement's intensified interest in the self. The theme of the book, "the needs of the person are the needs of the planet," reverberates throughout the text. The first part of the books is titled the "Manifesto of the Person," perhaps in conscious juxtaposition to *The Communist Manifesto*, which for the left has always signified the elevation of the working class as a group, not as individuals. Thus, for the counterculture, technological issues, problems, and solutions are defined in individualist rather than in social terms.

ALTERNATIVE TECHNOLOGY AND THE CRITIQUE OF COMMUNICATION TECHNOLOGIES

The counterculture's shift away from the establishment of an alternative social structure to the alternative organization of private, everyday life is reflected in attitudes that alternative technologists hold regarding communication technologies. According to Roszak (1978), the goal of communication, the "paradigm that would suit the needs of ecology," is "that of personal communication: mind reaching out to mind, intention impinging upon intention." Roszak's devil is mechanism. For him, the mechanistic model of nature upon which science is based is responsible for the creation of technologies that cannot capture "the experience of the personality in nature" (p. 58).

Technologies serve a society based on the goals of personal growth and fulfillment to the extent that they contribute to this kind of person-to-person, "natural" communication. Communication technologies are measured, therefore, by their ability to contribute to personal growth and fulfillment as well as to interpersonal communication. Generally, the distinction is black-and-white. Technologies either do or don't—can or can't—contribute to this personal growth and communication. Illich (1973), for example, labels technologies as either convivial or anticonvivial. Convivial technologies (or tools) are those that foster self-realization, those that "give each person who uses them the greatest opportunity to enrich the environment with the fruits of his or her vision" (p. 22). Anticonvivial technologies (or manipulative tools), by contrast, cannot be easily used by anyone and cannot provide the user with a channel for self-expression and self-realization. These tools impose their use on people. Anticonvivial tools master the individual; the individual does not master the tool.

Illich claims to focus his analysis on the structure of tools, not their use. But herein lies a serious ambiguity in his argument. He hints that, in the case of some tools, their structure alone determines their nature. Questions of use, ownership, and control are irrelevant when Illich insists that, "Certain tools are destructive no matter who owns them" (p. 27). Yet the thrust of his argument is about the use of tools, not their structures. Size, technical sophistication, institutional organization, and degree of centralization are not the distinguishing factors in determining whether a tool is convivial or anticonvivial. Convivial tools may be large, and their production and control may be highly centralized. The only distinguishing factor is the tool's usefulness in enhancing personal growth and fulfillment and interpersonal communication. Thus, for example, Illich declares that the telephone is convivial. Why?

Anybody can dial the person of his choice if he can afford a coin. . . . The telephone lets anybody say what he wants to the person of his choice; he can conduct business, express love, or pick a quarrel. It is impossible for bureaucrats to define what people say to each other on the phone, even though they can interfere with—or protect—the privacy of their exchange (p. 23).

Likewise, the alphabet, cheap paper, the pen, the pencil, the typewriter, and copying devices are convivial tools because they "deprofessionalized the recorded word." The tape recorder and the camera are convivial tools because they promote "interactive communication" (p. 69).

This confusion regarding the unit of analysis is integrally related to Illich's definition of tools. And it is a confusion with serious consequences for critiquing the relationship between technology and society. Illich defines tools as both physical machines and social arrangements, either of which may be convivial or anti-convivial. Thus, even though the tape recorder and the camera are convivial tools, they may be put in the service of manipulative institutions. "The manipulative nature of institutions and schooling for the acceptance of manipulation have put these ideally convivial tools at the service of more one-way teaching" (p. 69). Teaching, or schooling, is here an anticonvivial tool. Illich seriously obfuscates his own distinction between the structure of tools and their use. Schooling, a tool, actually uses another tool, in this case the tape recorder and camera. By focusing on schooling in the case of considering the conviviality of the tape recorder and the camera, Illich clearly concerns himself more with questions of the use, and not really the structure, of tools. Illich's emphasis on use is understandable, given his conception of a tool with a singular nature. After all, of what consequence is writing about the singular nature of a tape recorder or camera when the issue of more political and social consequence is the nature of institutions (as tools) that use the tools in divergent ways?

The obfuscation of the distinction between structure and use and the resulting emphasis on use—coupled with the notion that tools ought to serve personal growth, fulfillment, and interpersonal communication—dominate the Alternative Technology movement. As a whole, this very emphasis undercuts the claims that Alternative Technology can provide a powerful critique of, and alternative to, modern corporate-developed technologies. The movement tends to affirm the development of modern technology, as long as the technology can be seen as being in some way capable of enhancing personal growth and development. In addition, in the process of affirming such technologies, the movement even contributes to streamlining modern technological development in service of industrial productivity!

Illich's program for change calls for public ownership of resources and of the means of production, along with public control over the determination of the structure and use of modern tools. Nevertheless, there is evident in Illich's work (though it is less evident in Illich's than in the work of most alternative technologists) a disquieting and unsatisfactory conservative, uncritical position toward the analysis of modern technology. To begin with, Illich expresses the belief that technological growth has allowed us to develop a society that is now capable of using convivial tools. While he at once lauds the development of modern technology, he falls prey to the ideology of industrialization: "Tools for a convivial and yet efficient society could not have been designed at an earlier stage of history. We now can design the machinery for eliminating slavery without enslaving man to the machine" (p. 35).

The excitement generated by the computer within the Alternative Technology movement provides a particularly significant example of the general and uncritical acceptance of modern communication technologies. One would hardly expect the Alternative Technology movement to latch onto the computer as a liberating technology, but it has done just that. In an interesting exchange between two alternative technologists in *Peace News for Nonviolent Revolution,* Jan Wallis (1977) maintains that computers need not be the handmaidens of increased centralized decision making. Rather, she depicts the computer's potential for storage and retrieval as a useful tool for information sharing and the decentralization of decision making. She posits a free flow of information that will give everyone relevant input in order to promote meaningful, informed decision making. Thus, ideally, the computer can conform to the goals of the counterculture by supporting the reorganization of work into small, autonomous, but linked collectives.[1]

In response to Wallis' article, Mike Cavanagh (1977) criticizes Wallis' conception of the computer system, but he argues similarly that the computer can be made to conform to the goals and values of the counterculture. They differ only slightly, and only in regard to the size of the computer and to the way the computer should be used and controlled. Cavanagh objects to Wallis' reliance on the conception of computer systems as large, centralized computing facilities. Labeling this type of computer system the "consumer computer," he argues that, since it is the product of a consumer society, it can serve only a consumer society. Counterculture computers, he maintains, should be small and used not to create vast interconnected communication networks but to aid users in the performance of otherwise dull tasks.

Despite their differences, both Wallis and Cavanagh believe that the computer can be "liberated," that it can be used to serve the goals of the counterculture. Cavanagh states the position eloquently:

The computer is a powerful tool which may be used either to oppress or liberate. If we turn our backs on technology and leave it to the forces of destruction they may well destroy us all. By liberating the computer we may also take a step towards the liberation of our own consciousness (p. 15).

That sense of being compelled to adopt and adapt the computer, as indicated in Cavanagh's remarks, pervades the Alternative Technology movement. The Spring 1979 issue of the *Journal of Community Communications,* titled "Taking Control of Technology" (1979), is largely devoted to the issue of the relationship between computer technologies and social change. Most of the articles discourse on the use and misuse of computers, but the option of not using the computer is never considered. The editor of the issue, Sandy Emerson (1979, p. 1), indicates that the emphasis on use and misuse reflects the simple fact that "computers, particularly small, cheap computers, are currently at the forefront of new developments in communications technology." Apparently, the computer dominates the forefront of countercultural developments in communication just as much as it dominates the forefront in corporate developments in communication. The counterculture's fascination with the computer leads naturally to much more discussion of the possible uses of the technology than to critical analysis of the larger generalized relationship between the technology and society.

THE CO-OPTATION OF ALTERNATIVE TECHNOLOGY

An even more troubling characteristic of the Alternative Technology movement's approach to the computer, as well as to technology in general, is that, by lauding technological developments and adapting them to the movement's uses, the movement contributes significantly to the health of just that system of corporate domination that it initially reacted against. Sadly, but bluntly stated, the movement is easily co-opted.

The tendency for the technology and technical systems developed by the counterculture to be co-opted by corporate interests has become obvious even to alternative technologists. Writes one alternative technologist in *Peace News for Nonviolent Revolution* (Elliot, 1979, p. 12), "Alternative technology used to be, for many people, the key to a better society. Recently, however, industry and government have managed to take up the products, or hardware, of AT [Alternative Technology], whilst conveniently ignoring the software, the social, political and economic ideas which gave rise to AT."

Nowhere has the co-optation of Alternative Technology been more dramatic than in the development of solar energy in the United States. *The Sun Betrayed: A Study of the Corporate Seizure of U.S. Solar Energy Development,* a study conducted by Ray Reece (1979, see pp. 163–189), chronicles the way in which the "small is beautiful" solar technology has been, and continues to be, co-opted by larger firms, which have been able to exercise dominance over the smaller endeavors of the Alternative Technology movement. The larger firms have been able to establish their dominance by diversifying, by relying on government subsidization, and simply by squeezing out smaller endeavors. Once these larger firms exercise control over the solar hardware, they further develop the technology in accordance with their own large scale, highly centralized, mass-produced and mass-consumed, profit-oriented mode of production, a mode that is diametrically opposed to the liberatory goals of the Alternative Technology movement.

A similar exploitation of alternative communication technologies can and does occur—although perhaps less dramatically at present. For example, it has been pointed out that a major goal of CYBERSYN, a computer system developed in Allende's Chile, which was intended to play an integral role in socialist reconstruction, was "to render workers' participation and control increasingly effective by constructing a technological framework for the self-management of society" (Athanasiou, 1979, pp. 9–10).[2] But this system was merely and easily taken over and put into use by the Chilean secret police after the 1973 coup and the fall of the Allende regime.

CYBERSYN was designed to allow for a high degree of autonomous local participation, or decentralism, while at the same time permitting the kind of centralism that was essential to allow for national monitoring and planning. Tom Athanasiou, in analyzing the CYBERSYN system, maintains that while there would likely have been some conflicts between the system and the working class, even if there had not been a coup, the system was generally complementary to the goals and values of the revolution, which was characterized by worker control and participation.

Once the system was taken over by the Chilean secret police, who knows to what use it might have been put? With the ability to monitor at the local level and plan at the national level, the technology seems dangerously capable of being adapted to a flow in the opposite direction. Instead of input and control coming from workers, such a computer system might just as easily be used to monitor and exercise control over the workers.

Alternative technologists typically take the position that such assimilation is not the fault of the technology. Stephanie Klein (1979), for example, sees it as ironic that a system such as the British Post Office's Prestel system (or Viewdata), which was designed with the potential to facilitate interactive public information and control over the processes and production of goods, could so easily conform to the tendency of the marketplace to provide one-way consumer information. Yet she explicitly defends the belief that, "The technology of Prestel is not the limiting factor in its use; it is the social context in which it exists" (p. 18).

But co-optation occurs not only at the level of assimilating systems for alternative uses, but also at the level of marketing. The new, alternative technologies emphasize home and personal uses. By marketing complementary technologies, corporate enterprises further expand their more traditional dominance and control over technology in industry and business to communities, homes, and personal lives. Until quite recently, for example, the market for computers has been limited to business and industry. Yet as the small home and community computers become more popular and workable, thanks in part to the innovativeness of the Alternative Technology movement, a new market for new products is opened up for corporate enterprise. Further, we can expect that these corporate adaptations of the alternative technologies and systems will conform to the goals and values of the corporations that produce them. The computers are likely to be more "consumer computers." In her commentary on Prestel, Klein (1979, p. 18) notes that the computer system, in concordance with the general tendencies of the marketplace, tends "to take over more and more functions which were formerly performed by families and communities for themselves." As technologies are more and more co-opted and produced by larger corporate interests, the more our home and community life can be defined—if not controlled—by the corporate interests. The Alternative Technology movement ultimately provides these corporate interests with new products, new markets, and new marketing strategies.

CONCLUSION

In terms of its ability to critique the relationship between communication technologies and society, Alternative Technology makes tremendous strides over Technology Assessment. The critique recognizes that technologies must be understood in terms of their social roles. Where Technology Assessment focuses on side effects, Alternative Technology focuses on the integral relationship between technologies and social organization, structure, and values. A critique of technologies necessarily involves a critique of the society that uses them.

The critique remains inadequate, however, due to the movement's fascination with technology, a fascination that tends to cloud the ability to comprehend the full range of complexity operative in the relationship between technology and society. This fascination is an only thinly veiled commitment to the equation of technological growth and social progress. Intrigued—even compelled—by the desire to liberate modern communication technologies, Alternative Technology focuses on the variable uses of technologies. This focus on use tends to ignore the structure of the technologies and the extent to which those structures are integral to the social relations of production responsible for their appearance.

Intervention based on this model of the relationship between technology and society fails to address that relationship beyond questions of use. Intervention tends not only to ignore the question (or possibility) of shaping the social roots of invention and innovation, but also tends to accept the structure of technologies as readily adaptable.

Alternative Technology does not support unchallenged modern technological development to the extent that Technology Assessment does. However, the movement's emphasis on use has rendered its interventions largely ineffectual and easily co-opted by exactly that which it decries. What is still needed—what neither Technology Assessment nor Alternative Technology has provided—is a critique of the relationship between technology and society that can imbed invention and the structure of technologies, as well as their use, in the social fabric. Only then would intervention respond to and address the true complexity of those relationships. Luddism, as discussed in the next chapter, begins to consider more directly the ways in which the invention and structure of technologies, as well as their use, are integrally related to social structure.

FOOTNOTES

[1] Wallis' analysis of the computer as facilitating decision making is a popularly argued position within the Alternative Technology movement in support of the computer as an alternative tool. It is interesting to note, however, the degree to which the rationale used is merely a reworking of the classical liberal conception of man as a rational animal, a reworking that reflects a reliance on the ideology of industrialization as a measure of

human nature. Both the classical liberal and reworked versions of this approach characterize humans as rational decision makers, wanting only appropriate information upon which to base rational decisions. The problem with humans, and society, as implied by the reworked version, is that decision makers tend to make *inefficient* decisions. But the computer can resolve this problem by providing information more efficiently.

[2] The following description of CYBERSYN drawns on Athanasiou (1979).

---

chapter four

Luddism

Unlike Technology Assessment, Luddism is neither an approach nor a set of methods. Unlike Alternative Technology, Luddism is not a movement (though it once was). Luddism is really a spirit—a spirit that is suspicious of the very structure of certain technologies. Some technologies are, to the Luddite, inherently evil, and no alteration of their uses can alter their evil nature. Consequently, Luddism is also, in spirit, genuinely suspicious of the equation of technological growth and social progress. If some technologies are inherently evil, they can do nothing other than retard social progress.

The spirit of Luddism, however, involves more than just a suspicion of the structures of technologies. It also involves a realization that the structures of technologies are integrally related to the social structures within which they emerge. Thus, the structures themselves reflect the economic, political, and cultural structure of society.

The term "Luddite" is normally used pejoratively. It is used to refer to the "thoughtless" destruction of technologies—the desire to "halt" progress by halting or curbing technological development. When compared with Technology Assessment or Alternative Technology, Luddism is decidedly activist: Its interventionist goals are consciously directed much more to limiting, curbing, or controlling technological development than to aiding, streamlining, or adapting it. Yet beneath the rhetoric of destruction and despair that characterizes the Luddite spirit lies a far more sophisticated understanding of the relationship between technology and society than Technology Assessment or Alternative Technology have been able to offer.

Luddism is, however, a complex phenomenon, and the suspicion of the structure of technologies and of their relationships to the structure of society has taken many forms. By examining first the historical roots of Luddism and by considering the complex motivations of the Luddite movement, we can better understand what it means to label someone a "contemporary Luddite." Contemporary Luddites advance a unique sense of the relationship between technology and society, and their model for intervention in that relationship, despite its limitations, comes closer to responding to the real relationships between communication technologies and society than do Technology Assessment and Alternative Technology.

HISTORICAL LUDDISM

The name "Luddites" was first given to a group of workers in Lancashire, England, who rioted and destroyed stocking frames in 1811. The destruction was a deliberate policy on the part of the group, which was demanding work, higher pay, and better working conditions. The destruction of machines spread to neighboring districts between 1811 and 1817, and eventually the label was used to describe any number of machine breakers, thieves, murderers, reformers, and revolutionaries (Thomis, 1972; Thompson, 1963, 552–602).

Generally, the term "Luddism" is equated with machine breaking, although the Luddites were not the first—or last—group to engage in such destruction. Eric Hobsbawm (1952) has traced machine breaking to the earliest phases of the Industrial Revolution, and currently historians label any incidence of machine breaking as "Luddism" (Thomis, 1972, 12).

Of the many possible motives for machine breaking, Hobsbawm (1952) identifies two that figured prominently in the machine breaking of the eighteenth and nineteenth centuries. The first motive involves a particular hostility toward the machine itself. The machines of the Industrial Revolution—particularly those with labor-saving characteristics—were often seen as the cause of unemployment, of a lower standard of living for workers, and of the subjection of the rhythms of work to the rhythms of the machines. Workers often placed the blame for these changes in the social relations of production on the machines themselves and they expressed their hostility by destroying the machines.

The second motive for machine breaking that Hobsbawm identifies involves hostility not particularly toward the machines, but rather toward the owners of the machines, that is, the capitalists. As Hobsbawm points out, machine breaking was an established, traditional form of worker protest in England—particularly in mining and manufacturing—in an era without established unions. Besides machines, workers would destroy the capitalists' property and goods. This kind of "collective bargaining by riot" was often quite effective.

During the period of the Luddite movement, unemployment was particularly high, food was scarce, and poverty was widespread. The prevailing popular view of the Luddites is that they were motivated to destroy machines because they were convinced that the new machines were responsible for their woes and, in particular, for putting them out of work (see, for example, Berry, 1970). Often, in fact, the Luddites are characterized as wanton, unruly, thieving bandits, engaged in pointless violence. In this scenario, the hostility is directed toward the machine, not the capitalist.

Recently, however, historians have argued that the primary motivations of the Luddite movement were far more political and far more calculated to strike a blow against the capitalist and the capitalist system rather than against the machine itself (Hobsbawm, 1952; Thomis, 1972; Thompson, 1963, 552–602). E. P. Thompson (1963), in an examination of the Luddite movement, emphasizes the movement's political nature. He concludes that while the movement began by using machine breaking as a form of collective bargaining, it was driven steadily in a more insurrectionary direction and eventually "trembled on the edge of ulterior revolutionary objectives (p. 553).

CONTEMPORARY LUDDISM AND
THE CRITIQUE OF COMMUNICATION TECHNOLOGIES

The groups to be labeled in this section as "contemporary Luddites," with respect to communication technologies, do not engage in the physical act of machine breaking. They do, however, in spirit, resemble the Luddites in some important respects. The first broad category of contemporary Luddites is made up of those who are motivated by hostility toward the technologies, not toward the owners of the technologies or toward the structure of their ownership. Some proponents of this position can be labeled almost as easily as alternative technologists, but the subtle distinction lies in *the emphasis on the complete rejection of entire classes or groups of technologies, no matter who owns or controls them.* Thus, for example, the Luddite response to computer technology is simply that it ought not to be employed.

Andy Gates (1977), for example, takes a strongly Luddite position on computer technology when he writes that he has "doubts about using computers in any context. These are connected with my doubts about the implications of using so-called 'high technology' in general" (p. 14). For Gates, the computer can never be used to facilitate human decision making, for, "If all the factors to be taken into account in making a decision could be expressed in formulae that a computer can handle, it would produce the decision or model that fitted those formulae most exactly" (p. 14). Nor can the computer aid people in taking control of their own lives, for the specialized languages employed require considerable expertise to use, and, even if everyday language is employed, those languages are just as likely to be limiting ("is anyone going to bother with plain Welsh?"). Furthermore, Gates argues, programming will always be, of necessity, a limiting activity. Programmers, by necessity, will exercise power over the people who use the system.

The Luddite rejection of the machines of modern communication, as represented by Gates' argument, is not a particularly pervasive or consequential contemporary response to technological growth. A far more formidable response is that represented by authors often labeled the "pessimists" or "prophets of doom."[1] Lewis Mumford (1963, 1967, 1970), Jacques Ellul (1964, 1973), and Herbert Marcuse (1941, 1964) best represent this group. While there are substantial differences among the three writers, they all make serious attempts to analyze technology as it is imbedded in the social fabric. To varying degrees, each of these authors recognizes and explores connections between the machines and the social environment. They are all contemporary Luddites because they all condemn the modern machines as well as the social structure of which the machines are a part.

The particular stengths of this position lie precisely in its ability to demonstrate the degree to which technologies are a product of the social environment. In particular, Mumford's historical analyses of the relationship between the inner dynamics of various technologies and the societies that have produced them are instructive. For example, in *Technics and Civilization* Mumford (1963) considers the invention and innovation of the clock. Mumford maintains that a device for the regular measurement of time came into being only when the environment demanded it. As the need and desire to maintain a regular and orderly routine arose, so did the need for a device to measure, if not create, time. Mumford traces the origins of the first clocks to the monasteries of the West. He writes:

Within the walls of the monastery was sanctuary: under the rule of the order surprise and doubt and caprice and irregularity were put at bay. Opposed to the erratic fluctuations and pulsations of the worldly life was the iron discipline of the rule. Benedict added a seventh period to the devotions of the day, and in the seventh century, by a bull of Pope Sabinianus, it was decreed that the bells of the monastery be rung seven times in the twenty-four hours. These punctuation marks in the day were known as the canonical hours, and some means of keeping count of them and ensuring their regular repetition became necessary (p. 13).

The clock was thus developed to manage time. Mumford concludes: "The monastery was the seat of a regular life, and an instrument for striking the hours at intervals or for reminding the bell-ringer that it was time to strike the bells, was an almost inevitable product of this life" (p. 13). The very structure of this technology, its essential nature, reflects not only the structure of society but the elevation of the value of accuracy, standardization and, indirectly, the elevation of the objectivity of science. Mumford claims that "by its essential nature it dissociated time from human events and helped create the belief in an independent world of mathematically measurable sequences: the special world of science" (p. 15).

Regrettably, a serious shortcoming accompanies the contemporary Luddite sense of the relationship between technologies and the social environment within which they arise. The shortcoming, as was the case in Alternative Technology, has to do with a definition of technology. Only in this case, the problem is the utter reduction of the terms "technology" and "society" to a single dynamic. The object of study becomes a singular dynamic, and every thing, thought, and concept is reducible to it.

Mumford's definition of "the machine" is generally accepted as the appropriate definition of the object of study within this group. Machines remains the term to specify particular objects, such as a printing press. Yet the machine, and not machines, is the real object of study. The machine is used as a "shorthand reference to the entire technological complex. This will embrace the knowledge and skills and arts derived from industry or implicated in the new technics, and will include various forms of tool, instrument, apparatus and utility as well as machines proper" (Mumford, 1963, p. 12). The machine, or "technics"—the real object of study—thus becomes an all-inclusive term. For Marcuse (1941, p. 414), "technology"—used synonomously with technics—is defined in a similarly all-inclusive way:

Technology, as a mode of production, as a totality of instruments, devices and contrivances which characterize the machine age is thus at the same time a mode of organizing and perpetuating (or changing) social relationships, a manifestation of prevalent thought and behavior patterns, an instrument for control and domination.

Ellul (1964) uses the term "technique," but the meaning is essentially the same: *"technique* is the *totality of methods rationally arrived at and having absolute efficiency* (for a given stage of development) in *every* field of human activity" (p. xxv).

Serious limitations result from thus defining the machine, technic, and technique. First, it draws attention to a single social dynamic and defines all of society in terms of that single dynamic. For Ellul, as an example, all of modern society can be characterized by the predominance of technique. While Ellul characterizes machines as initially responsible for the development of technique, technique has taken on an essentially inertial power to integrate itself into and transform society. Technique "constructs the kind of world the machine needs and introduces order where the incoherent banging of machinery heaped up ruins. It clarifies, arranges, and rationalizes; it does in the domain of the abstract what the machine did in the domain of labor. It is efficient and brings efficiency to everything" (1964, p. 5). In our present age, technique has universally exercised control over all of human existence. It is the one dynamic that defines human existence: "in our civilization technique is in no way limited. It has been extended to all spheres and encompasses every activity, including human activities. . . . Technique has been extended geographically so that it covers the whole earth" (1964, p. 78).

There is a complete confluence in this notion of technique among values, social structure, and technology. We, as naive victims of technique, might not be able to recognize the confluence and the resulting control over our lives, but it is always there, just below the surface of appearances, to exert domination. As Marcuse (1941, p. 429) argues, "Underneath the complicated web of stratified control is an array of more or less standardized techniques, tending to one general pattern, which ensure the material reproduction of society."

The consequence of utilizing this kind of approach in analyzing the relationship between communication technologies and society is best illustrated in the study of propaganda by Ellul (1973). The preindustrial, pretechnological era is, for Ellul, a kind of Golden Age. It was a time when each individual was closely related with other individuals in primary groups through direct interpersonal relations and communications. These primary groups are seen as being "spontaneously democratic. . . . leadership . . . is recognized spontaneously," and individuals within the group are considered free (p. 100). Humankind loses this innocence with the rise of technique, which accompanies the twentieth century technoindustrial society. Small cohesive groups, such as the family and the church, break up, and the traditional social structure disintegrates. The problem of the possibility of communication becomes crucial, and forms of mass media are developed that introduce a new kind of communication in the now-fragmented society. These mass media make it possible for propaganda to exist. The breakdown of primary groups leaves individuals alienated from themselves and from one another in a fragmented and "mass-ified" society. Individuals, in their dissipated state, need something to fill their empty and frustrating lives. So they turn to propaganda, which essentially defines the modern forms of communication. Thoroughly propagandized, the people cannot be governed by any other means, and thus even the state is "burdened with the task of acting through propaganda" (p. 128). Progaganda, like technique, is a total system that can be accepted or rejected only in its entirety. Yet in a modern propagandized society, turning back is impossible, given the impoverished state of the individual.

As this example of Ellul illustrates, these Luddites condemn not only the technologies but the entire social system of which the technologies are an integral part. The social system and its technologies are nearly completely reduced to a single dynamic—be that dynamic labeled "the machine," "technique," or "domination." The position allows for no social, economic, or cultural conflict or contradictions of any consequence, and it assumes complete confluence between the dynamic and the nature and use of communication technologies. Admitting no possibility of contradiction, it is therefore condemned to a pessimism of such proportions as to be very nearly paralyzing when it comes to providing a basis for intervention.

LUDDITE OPTIONS FOR INTERVENTION

The blanket condemnation of a dynamic that defines all of society inhibits the ability to criticize particular aspects of unique relationships between technologies and society. If the dynamic—the technique or the machine—is undesirable, everything that characterizes society and its technologies must logically be undesirable as well. The logical purview for intervention is then the total alteration or destruction of the dynamic, and thus the destruction of the total social structure and its technologies. Yet how does one destroy the dynamic that underlies an entire social structure? Where does one begin? By condemning an entire system as uniformly and cohesively undesirable, where will the motivation and agent of change arise?

Clearly, the motivation and change agent cannot come from the inhabitants of the society, for if they are truly part of an homogeneous society defined by technique or the machine, they surely cannot escape its clutches. There can be no escape. For Ellul, the inhabitants of this society, whose very culture is identified with propaganda and technique, lack the will, the desire, and the capability to effectively alter the propagandized technocratic society. While Mumford's earlier position, as illustrated in *Technics and Civilization* (1963), reveals optimistic hopes that the situation is rectifiable, his later works become increasingly more resigned to believing that humankind is incapable of "throwing off the myth of the machine" (1970, especially pp. 414–435). The logic of the position renders it exceeding difficult to escape a withdrawal into a pessimism so complete that it is absolutely incapable of providing a strategy for effective intervention.

The Luddite intervention that is characterized by a condemnation of the machine, as discussed earlier, fails to understand critically the nature of the relationship between the technologies and the social structure—particularly that technologies arise within a social structure and are defined and shaped by it. Intervention based on this approach is thereby inadequate, for destroying technologies does not begin to address the question of the forces that created them. Yet neither can the Luddite response that recognizes an integral relationship between technologies and social structure provide a basis for adequate intervention. Because this perspective so totally denies the existence of dynamic contradiction and conflict, it obscures the nature of the relationship between communication technologies and social structure, reduces it to mere reflection or confluence, and inhibits the possibility for meaningful and effective intervention.

CONCLUSION

Clearly, a new perspective on the relationship between communication technologies and social structure is warranted, particularly if it is to provide the basis for effective intervention in that relationship. Technology Assessment cannot provide the tools for rising to such a task, for as has been demonstrated, Technology Assessment is merely one aspect of the management of technological development. Neither can Alternative Technology suffice as a model for analysis and critique. In spite of Alternative Technology's apparent promise, its fascination with technology and its emphasis on personal use cloud its vision with respect to the relationship between technology and society, thus retarding its ability and willingness to say "no" to technological development. Likewise, the Luddite response that can see only the machines as the cause cannot contribute the tools to examine the way in which those technologies emerge as part of the social structure. Finally, the Luddite response that homogenizes technology and culture into one uniform conception of technique cannot be utilized to analyze the complexities of society, the technologies it produces, and the varieties of uses to which the technologies may be put.

The only hope we have for discovering the complex nature of the relationship between communication technologies and society is to develop a contemporary critical approach to technology. This approach must strive to analyze technologies as integral, though derivative, parts of a complex social structure. To develop such an approach, we must set aside the fascination with technology and the equation of technological development and progress that characterize Technology Assessment and Alternative Technology. As Langdon Winner (1977b) has argued, the criticism of technology must be characterized by a willingness to say "no" to some technologies. Yet doing so is not necessarily a call to destroy technologies or to halt further innovation; rather it is a demand that "the notion of improving the human condition be clearly distinguished from technological innovation and removed from the contemporary fascination with technique and extraordinary apparatus" (p. 374).

Thus, we must be willing to examine technology and to evaluate its contribution to society. Yet we must also recognize that the technology is a product of society, not in the same homogeneous sense that the "pessimists" tend to see it, but in the everyday operation of a complex social structure where there is conflict and contradiction in the political, economic, legal, and cultural spheres. Only then will intervention be based on a sound knowledge of the relationship between the technology and the political, economic, and cultural complexities of which the technology is but a part.

FOOTNOTES

[1] For a discussion and critique of these labels, see Winner (1977a), pp. 52–57.

section two

The Relationship Between Communication Technologies and Society: Causality and Intervention

Technology Assessment, Alternative Technology, and Luddism each embody attitudes toward, and beliefs about, technologies and technological development. The previous section presented some of the ways in which these beliefs and attitudes were manifest in the range of technological intervention appropriate to each position. Also shown was that neither Technology Assessment, Alternative Technology, nor Luddism was able to provide adequate tools for analyzing the relationship between communication technologies and society and for guiding satisfactory, critical technological intervention.

Fundamental to the inadequacies of each of these positions is the implicit (sometimes explicit) utilization of deficient conceptions of the causal relationship between technologies and society. By exploring the inadequacies of these underlying conceptions of causality, we might comprehend the ways in which the limitations of each position are "fixed" at the level of theory. Conceptions of causality provide parameters within which a variety of related responses can, and does, occur. Iron-

49

ically, widely divergent judgments on the merits of technological development often operate with essentially identical conceptions of causality.

Inadequate conceptions of causality underlie not only inadequate analyses of the relationship between communication technologies and society, but also the kinds of intervention that emanate from those analyses. Once this link between theory, analysis, and intervention is elucidated, it becomes obvious that responsible technological intervention requires an alternative conception of causality. The proposed alternative is a conception of causality as structural, a notion based in large part on the work of Louis Althusser. To accentuate the viability of such a conception, this section explores the ways in which the three currently dominant conceptions of causality—simple, symptomatic, and expressive—circumscribe the analysis of the relationship between communication technologies and society, and thereby of technological intervention.[1] Then explored are the ways in which structural causality offers a viable alternative to these positions. The focus in particular is on the way in which a conception of causality as structural promotes a more critical understanding of the relationship between communication technologies and society. Consequently, technological intervention based on this critical understanding can—unlike Technology Assessment, Alternative Technology, and Luddism—address truly significant aspects of the relationship between communication technologies and society.

Beginning with a precise definition of cause, causality, effect, and effectivity is difficult, because the range of traditionally acceptable—or debatable—definitions has emerged from within the traditions that are here largely rejected. In general, a *cause* is that which produces a change; and the *change,* or *effect,* can be explained in terms of the cause (Taylor, 1967, 56). According to *Webster's Third New International Dictionary, causality* is the term used to describe the relationship between the cause and the effect. The problem with these definitions is that their simplicity already embodies a view of causality as mechanistic. Thinking of causality in such simple terms makes it difficult to appreciate the alternatives offered by expressive and structural causality. The term "effectivity" will therefore often be used rather than "cause" "effect," or "causality," in order to encourage thinking about the processes of change in terms that are not so evidently mechanistic.

Unfortunately, equally simple definitions of causality that capture the processes of effectivity in expressive and structural causality are not possible. This is especially difficult for structural causality. Only in the process of an arduous rethinking of what are for the most part deep-seated prejudices—and an equally arduous attempt to explore a new way of thinking—might we sense what it means to talk about effectivity as structural. Such an understanding may be possible only with what is

———

often referred to in the physical sciences as "hand waving." By talking about, talking around, presenting examples, and by comparing structural causality with rejected positions, structural causality will hopefully come alive as a vital alternative to more traditional ways of thinking about causality.

FOOTNOTES

[1] The terms "simple causality" and "symptomatic causality" are variations of terms used by Williams (1975, 10–14). The term "expressive causality" is derived from Althusser & Balibar (1977, 186–187).

chapter five

Mechanistic Conceptions of Causality: Simple and Symptomatic Causality

More than any other conception of causality considered in this section, simple and symptomatic causality—have roots that run deep in Western philosophy, in the philosophy of science, and in mathematics. Virtually any of the myriad of books and articles written about causality in the Western tradition will discuss the work of philosophers, scientists, and mathematicians such as Democritus, Aristotle, Descartes, Hume, Newton, J. S. Mill, Mach, A. J. Ayer, and C. J. Ducasse. Relevant philosophical orientations include a similarly broad range of traditions, such as atomism, mechanism, empiricism, and positivism. The conception of causality, however, that links these positions, not the variations in and between them, is of interest here.[1] These positions share a "mechanistic conception of causality," a conception that has shaped most of Western thinking about the relationship between technology and society. This broad categorization is further broken down into simple and symptomatic causality, because at the level of technological intervention, a variation within the larger tradition suggests significantly different kinds of activities. Both positions share, however, the most basic tenets of the mechanistic conception of causality: *that causes and effects are discrete and isolated objects, events, or conditions that exercise effectivity externally.* Both the cause and the effect are self-contained and distinct from their environments, as is the cause–effect event. A cause is an autonomous phenomenon that has an effect on another phenomenon that is otherwise also autonomous. The world is divided into simple, discrete parts, which are essentially unrelated except, perhaps, for that moment when a cause produces an effect, after which the parts are again simple, discrete, and unrelated.

The origins of this orientation in modern philosophy are often attributed to Descartes. The second and third rules in Descartes's (1637/1960) "true method of obtaining knowledge of everything which my mind was capable of understanding" (p. 14) included the prescription to "divide each of the difficulties which I encountered into as many parts as possible, and as might be required for an easier solution," beginning "with the things which were simplest and easiest to understand, and gradually and by degrees reaching toward more complex knowledge, even treating, as though ordered, materials which were not necessarily so" (p. 15). The relationships between these isolated and simplest of things were to be examined in simple linear and mathematical terms:

> I realized that in order to understand the principles of relationships I would sometimes have to consider them singly, and sometimes comprehend and remember them in groups. I thought I could consider them better singly as relationships between lines, because I could find nothing more simple or more easily pictured to my imagination and my senses. But in order to remember and understand them better when taken in groups, I had to express them in numbers, and in the smallest numbers possible. Thus I took the best traits of geometrical analysis and algebra, and corrected the faults of one by the other (p. 16).

This bias toward mathematical explanation dominates philosophical enquiry into causal connections even today. Open any treatise on causality, and you will probably find that it is replete with equations, mathematical symbols, and a myriad of permutations of the basic schematic $C \rightarrow E$. Regardless of how a cause or effect is defined—as an event, property, condition, object, feature of an event, or class of events, or whatever—the mathematical depiction reinforces the conception of the cause and effect as discrete, isolated phenomena with no essential connection to their environments. Cause and effect, as depicted and conceived mathematically, can never be dialectically related. Though it is possible to draw arrows back and forth to indicate reciprocity, such as $C \rightleftarrows E$ or $C \longleftrightarrow E$, this reciprocity is still forever a simple linearity: C causes E; E then becomes C_2 which then causes E_2, and on and on. This process can be depicted in a simple linear fashion just as easily, such that $C_1 \cdot C_2 \cdots C_n \rightarrow E$ (Bunge, 1979, 121–122). I am in complete agreement with George Lukács (1972, 5–10) who argues that the numerical representation of phenomena reinforces an inability to glimpse the reality underlying a phenomenon, a reality that constitutes the relationship of the phenomenon to the larger social system or environment. The mathematical formulation encourages the artificial abstraction of something deemed "pure fact," as separable from its environment. Judging from contemporary philosophical debate on causality, the reality of the phenomena resides in their mathematical properties.

The epitome of the isolation of cause, effect, and context is achieved in the work of Hume, whose analysis of causation is considered by some to be the most influential Western model of causality. Hume's conception of causality is distinctive in that the isolation of cause and effect is so extreme that causality is reduced to mere convention. In *An Enquiry Concerning Human Understanding,* Hume (1955/1976) utilizes the illustration of one billiard ball striking another to make his argument. The one ball strikes the other, after which the struck ball is propelled forward. We can witness the conjunction of these two events, but, Hume argues, we can never know the relation between them. We can never be conscious of the power that renders the conjunction of the two events a connection. Hume argues that *"First,* it must be allowed that when we know a power, we know that very circumstance in the cause by which it is enabled to produce the effect, for those are supposed to be synonymous" (p. 53). Yet "All events," Hume subsequently insists, "seem entirely loose and separate. One event follows another, but we never can observe any tie between them. They seem *conjoined,* but never *connected"* (p. 59).

How then can we ever deem one phenomenon a cause and the other an effect? Hume argues that, after continually experiencing the conjunction, we *assume* connection. He writes:

But when one particular species of events has always, in all instances, been conjoined with another, we make no longer any scruple of foretelling one upon the appearance of the other, and of employing the reasoning which can alone assure us of any matter of fact or existence. We then call the one object "cause," the other "effect." We suppose that there is some connection between them, some power in the one by which it infallibly produces the other and operates with the greatest certainty and strongest necessity (pp. 59–60).

The attention in Hume's analysis of causation is therefore directed toward the constant conjunction of apparently isolated events, not toward the power or force that connects them. Both cause and effect are defined as objects to which we, by custom, impute connection. We can know the objects, but we can never develop a position that can "point out the circumstance in the cause which gives it a connection with its effect" (p. 61).

SIMPLE CAUSALITY AND ANALYSIS OF THE RELATIONSHIP BETWEEN COMMUNICATION TECHNOLOGIES AND SOCIETY

The Humean notion that conjunction does not equal connection plays only a minor role in the discussion of the causal relationship between

---

communication technologies and society. Only the most naive researchers argue that correlation (conjunction) equals causation (connection). Equally true, however, is that a significant amount of research merely imputes a cause when all that is really demonstrated is a conjunction. In fact, Hume argued that it is commonly the case that humans have an "idea" of a necessary connection between a cause and an effect—that is, that the cause compels the effect and that the appearance of the cause necessitates the effect (Hume, 1976, 61). Simple causality is characterized by this isolation of cause and effect in which the appearance of the cause necessitates specific effects. From this perspective, communication technologies are conceived of as autonomous causes whose appearance produces inevitable effects.

The classic representative of a simple causal position vis-à-vis communication technologies is Marshall McLuhan. McLuhan (McLuhan & Fiore, 1967) argues, for example, in *The Medium Is the Massage,* that writing "put an end to talk. It abolished mystery; it gave us architecture and town; it brought roads and armies, bureaucracy." Or elsewhere: "Print technology created the public. Electric technology created the mass. The public consists of separate individuals walking around with separate, fixed points of view. The new technology demands that we abandon the luxury of this posture, this fragmentary outlook." The effects wrought by the technologies of communication are, for McLuhan, entirely inevitable. He writes of the new electronic technology: "The instantaneous world of electric informational media involves all of us, all at once. No detachment or frame is possible." Or again: "Naturally, when electric technology comes into play, the utmost variety and extent of operations in industry and society quickly assume a unified posture."

Although McLuhan's position is an unusually explicit example of a simple causal position,the assumption of direct and unmediated effects of autonomous, isolated technologies abounds in studies of communication technologies. It is often argued that the telephone is the cause of both the growth of central cities and the urban sprawl that spelled their demise (see, for example, Moyer, 1977, 342–369). It has been suggested likewise that the telephone has encouraged the dissolution of the extended family, destroyed privacy, encouraged world peace, or, obversely, caused wars (see, for example, Brooks, 1975, 8).

These kinds of arguments are pervasive in studies of the relationship between communication technologies and society. Although these studies often contain valuable information, the causal framework within which they operate severely limits their explanatory powers. For example, they are absolutely incapable of explaining why some technologies are repressed or ignored, perhaps to reemerge later in the same society.

Such simple-minded conceptions of causality cannot explain—to use an example from outside communication—how the gun, which once flourished in Japanese warfare, could possibly have been abandoned and virtually forgotten (as it was), only to be resurrected over two hundred years later (Perrin, 1980). Nor can they explain why the Chinese, who although they had developed highly sophisticated printing technology, never developed printing to any significant extent (Fuhrmann, 1938, 25–29). Nor can McLuhan explain why the global village, the unified posture that industry and society were supposed to "quickly" assume with the appearance of electric technology, has yet to appear.

SIMPLE CAUSALITY
AND TECHNOLOGICAL INTERVENTION

A simple causal conception of the relationship between communication technologies and society lends itself well to two varieties of technological intervention: Luddism directed against the machine, and a particular strain of the Alternative Technology movement. Both of these positions share a common conception: that the desirable or undesirable effects of a technology are inherent in the technology itself. As long as the technology exists, the effects will necessarily occur. Thus, the only way to eliminate the effects is to eliminate the technology. The most obvious embodiment of this position is the Luddite intervention that is directed against the machine, as discussed in Chapter 4. Yet the Alternative Technology movement often betrays a similar tendency. When Illich (1973, p. 27) argues, for example, that certain tools are convivial or anticonvivial by "nature" and that "Certain tools are destructive no matter who owns them," he is positing the isolated, autonomous nature of certain technologies, as well as their ability to compel virtually unmediated effects.

The only kind of technological intervention that can be built on a simple conception of causality is—at best—saying "no" to a particular technology. Yet given the emphasis on inevitability, it is somewhat contradictory to assume that anyone has the power to turn the intellectually posed "no" into an actual intervention. Even given the theoretical possibility of acting on the "no," the overly simple conception of the causal connections between technologies and society renders it difficult to imagine how, in practical terms, one might intervene. The Luddite's smashing of the machines is the only really consistent model of behavior available.

SYMPTOMATIC CAUSALITY

In a critique of McLuhan's conception of causality, James Carey and John Quirk (1970, 398–399) point out that McLuhan fails to recognize that technologies have only potentials for effectivity, and that those potentials alone are not enough to insure the occurrence of particular effects. Social institutions may either thwart or enhance the potentials. Thus, Carey and Quirk argue, effects are not inherent in the technology itself. One must also look at the nature and role of social institutions for an explanation of the relationship between communication technologies and society. This corrective applied to the simple conception of causality—*the effectivity of institutional forces on the technology once it has appeared*—characterizes the second of the mechanical conceptions of causality: symptomatic causality. Although the characterization is still mechanistic—in that it persists in the implication that technologies are isolated, discrete, self-contained phenomena compelling effects in society—this position contributes an important mediation of those effects.

Symptomatic causality has a strong affinity to classical mechanics, in particular to classical physics as developed between the sixteenth and nineteenth centuries.[2] Classical mechanics, which reached its apex in Newton's laws of motion, concerns itself with quantitative laws that characterize the motion of discrete bodies through space. As summarized by David Bohm (1980, p. 35):

Newton's laws of motion imply that the future behavior of a system of bodies is determined completely and precisely for all time in terms of the initial positions and velocities of all the bodies at a given instant of time, and of the forces acting on the bodies. These forces may be *external forces,* which arise outside the system under investigation, or they may be *internal forces* of interaction between the various bodies that make up the system in question.

Newton's laws are generally applied within a system (such as the solar system). External forces are considered to be too small to be taken into account. The system itself is defined by the sum of those discrete causes, or forces, considered to be sufficient to explain the effects relevant to the way the system has been defined. Specifically, only the positions and velocities of the bodies within the system are used to determine the effects. The sum of these causes, the positions and velocities of all the bodies in the system at a given moment, are considered adequate to determine all future effects of all the bodies within the system.

The mechanistic attitude, which pervades the adoption of classical mechanics, assumes that the universe, at its most fundamental level, is composed of atoms or particles that obey certain causal laws. These atoms and the laws that govern them form the building blocks of all complexity and change within the universe. Any body can ultimately be explained in terms of fundamental fixed qualities. Each body behaves in a universally lawful manner and interacts with other bodies to generate lawful effects.

SYMPTOMATIC CAUSALITY AND ANALYSIS OF
THE RELATIONSHIP BETWEEN COMMUNICATION TECHNOLOGIES AND
SOCIETY

Although modern science—along with, for that matter, science since Newton—has moved far beyond the conception of causality prescribed by Newton, the popular conception that dominates the understanding of the relationship between communication technologies and society relies very heavily on a Newtonian model. Communication technologies are depicted first as external to the system, that is, they arise autonomously as isolated and discrete phenomena. Upon their appearance, they may enter into the system—in this case, a social system—which then acts on and with the technology so as to determine the effects of the technology. As opposed to the simple causal position, the technology does not initially bear any inherent effectivity. Once it has entered into the system and comes in contact with the social forces within that system, however, it becomes an effective force within the system—as that system has been narrowly defined. The technology provides a basis for a variety of social uses, but the particular forces that act on the technology shape its use for either good or evil purposes.

Although Lewis Mumford cannot be characterized as consistently depicting the relationship between technologies and society as symptomatic, much of his earlier work in particular expresses this position. In *Technics and Civilization* Mumford (1963, p. 6) writes:

No matter how completely technics relies upon the objective procedures of the sciences, it does not form an independent system, like the universe: it exists as an element in human culture and it promises well or ill as the social groups that exploit it promise well or ill. The machine itself makes no demands and holds out no promises: it is the human spirit that makes demands and keeps promises.

Mumford is arguing here that any technology is initially really autonomous. Technologies enter into the social system, where they are acted upon by social forces that, acting together as a catalyst, determine the technologies' effects.

This belief in the initial autonomy and neutrality of communication technologies is echoed by British sociologist, Robert Houlton (1973). Houlton maintains that communication systems alone determine nothing. Rather, they are subject to economic, social, and political interventions that arrange the systems in coherence with a particular society's institutions. Utilizing a symptomatic approach in a study of the American mass entertainment industry, Houlton attempts to demonstrate that the media are "open systems liable to chain reactions of intervention" (p. 119).

The belief in such autonomy and neutrality is implicit in many works that examine specific communication technologies. In an article on home video systems, Cliff Christians (1973) argues that "The media do not arise in a vacuum; but, as with all inventions, they are shaped dramatically by the societal structures in which they are created. . . . The history of communications systems reveals the large gap which inevitably develops between a new invention's potential and what is eventually done with it" (p. 231). Christians relates the history of the development of the home video system as an example of this gap between potential and actuality. He sees manufacturers turning to advertising as a certain and reliable source of revenue, and to that end shaping the system's programming to suit the needs of advertisers rather than developing the technology's more humanitarian potential. Christians depicts home video technology as initially autonomous and neutral. Only when the system's entrepreneurs adopt the marketing techniques of other media is a negative social effect imminent: "Contrary to predictions about radical transformation, this new communications idea is inevitably assuming the characteristics of other mass media systems" (p. 231). The ultimate illustration of Christians' belief in the autonomy of the technology is his faith that the same technology can be made to work for what he perceives as humanitarian goals as opposed to the goals of the capitalist market. He believes that "the business of those concerned with improving communications is to continue every effort to make the present system work. The focus of attention must be the advancement of broadcasting as we know it now" (p. 231).

One final example of the position that essentially autonomous and neutral technologies are shaped by society's institutions to suit the social order is a dominant attitude toward cable television. Ralph Lee Smith (1972), in *The Wired Nation*, decried the uses to which cable technology might be put. He argued that the technology was certain to be developed, but unless governmental action was taken, there was no way to insure that it would develop in a "desirable" way. Potentials were seen as limitless because the technology itself was considered neutral. Only social forces determine the nature of uses:

Under any circumstances, however, the cable will be built, and the aim must be, through positive policy and intelligent action, to take every advantage of its tremendous potentials for social good. . . . Finally, it should be remembered that the potential of cable for civic, community, educational, and cultural use is only beginning to be explored. There is almost limitless opportunity for creative action at the community level, that will contribute to making cable communications a valuable addition to urban life, and a tool for dealing with the problems and ills facing our nation and our society (pp. 98, 82).

SYMPTOMATIC CAUSALITY AND INTERVENTION

As these examples indicate, analyses based on symptomatic causality acknowledge that there is interaction between technologies and the social forces that put them to use, and that these forces shape the effects of the technologies. This recognition is an unquestionable advance over the simple causal position. Yet there are also some undesirable consequences of this position for the understanding of the causal relationship between communication technologies and society, and these consequences become most serious in the logic of intervention based on this approach. By positing the origins of a technology as initially outside the system, writers from this perspective totally disregard the way in which the technology may have been shaped by the system initially. For example, the invention of the technology is not considered to be integrally related to the system. To magnify the problem, however, by assuming that the only effects that the technology will have will come entirely from within the system as it shapes the uses of the technology, it makes no sense to say "no" to a particular technology. One need only intervene at the level of uses to insure desirable development. Thus, it does not occur to Smith, for example, to question the social choices responsible for the shape of cable technology; he merely assumes the technical shape. Smith (1972) only questions and seeks to control the specific implementation of cable: "When cable systems blanket major cities, cameras can be put everywhere. Everyone's comings and goings can be monitored every minute and hour of the day. Will this new form of police power be properly used? Should it be limited, and, if so, what should the limits be?" (p. 98). Similarly, it does not occur to Christians (1973) to question the forces responsible for the invention of home video systems and consider the ways in which those forces shaped the technology in the first place.

Most Technology Assessment is conducted with a conception of technology as related symptomatically to society. Although there often is a bow to the notion that some effects are inherent (a simple causal position), the real activity—the real intervention—occurs at the level of the ways the technology is put to work. So, for example, the National Academy of the Sciences argues that human behavior and institutions need to be adjusted to insure that technology is put to work in what it deems socially advantageous ways (U.S. Congress, 1969b, 15). As has been argued explicitly by Edward Dickson and Raymond Bowers (1974, p. 5):

A technology assessment appears to possess special utility when the technological innovation under consideration has begun to take a concrete form but has not yet been deployed or reached a critical concentration. Since it may take several years to go from pilot demonstration to wide-spread deployment there is ample time for deliberate policy decisions to affect the nature, regulation and deployment of the technology.

Similarly, Alternative Technology is for the most part firmly grounded in the belief that, if the control of technology is simply put in to the "proper" hands, any perceived negative effects can be controlled, and positive ones either enhanced or developed. As Dave Elliot (1979, p. 12) has written of the aspirations of the Alternative Technology movement: "The hope is that by developing our experience of local control over a wide range of decisions, and by creating de-central organisations we may be able to lay a base for—and ease the transition to—a more democratic society.

CONCLUSION

What Elliot ignores—and in fact what all adherents to a mechanistic conception of the causal relationship between communication technologies and society ignore—is that the very processes of invention and innovation are already deeply imbedded in the social fabric. Jacob Schmookler (1972), who has studied the process of technological innovation in industry extensively, concludes that, "Most new industrial technologies are found because they are sought" (p. 81). Similarly, Raymond Williams (1975, p. 14) maintains that any technology can be seen "as being looked for and developed with certain purposes and practices already in mind." If invention and innovation are already deeply imbedded in the social fabric, technologies can never be completely neutral or autonomous. If technologies are not neutral and autonomous, their effects cannot be totally determined by social interventions. Rather, the effectivity of a technology resides also in the degree to which the technology is itself an effect, the degree to which the values of the environment within which it was produced are imbedded in its very structure.

Intervention based on symptomatic analysis is therefore likely to be inadequate, as it precludes the possibility of acting in the relationship between technology and society prior to the technology's appearance. Expressive and structural causality, as discussed in the following chapters, conceptualize technologies as both causes and effects that are integrally related to the environment beginning with their inception. Each model also involves corresponding modes of intervention that emphasize acting in the relationship between technology and society before the appearance of technologies instead of simply "after the fact."

FOOTNOTES

[1] For a taste of the extent of the variations within the Western tradition of causality, see Bunge (1979).

[2] The discussion of classical mechanics is based largely on Bohm (1980), especially pp. 34–67, 130–136.

chapter six

Expressive Causality

Expressive causality contrasts sharply with the mechanistic conceptions of causality discussed in the previous chapter. From an expressive position, communication technologies are not discrete, autonomous objects whose effects are either inherent in them or the mere result of interaction with social forces. By contrast, an expressive position links technologies, as both cause and effect, to the society within which they emerge and exercise effectivity. Rather than technologies being isolatable phenomena, they are considered integral to the society as a whole.

To understand how technologies are integral and how effectivity flows between technologies and society, it is essential to understand the nature of "society as a whole." Expressive causality implies a particular vision of the social whole: *an expressive totality in which any and all phenomena are mere expressions of some inner essence, be that essence an idea, ideal, social configuration, or dynamic.* As the parts of the whole are merely expressions of the essence of the whole, everything is essentially reducible to that essence.

The relationship between the various parts of the totality and its essence is best captured by G. W. F. Hegel, whose entire philosophical edifice is built upon a notion of expressive totality. In *The Phenomenology of Mind,* Hegel (1967) posits the essence of the whole as something called "spirit" and describes the totality thus:

It is only spirit in its entirety that is in time, and the shapes assumed, which are specific embodiments of the whole spirit as such, present themselves in a se-quence one after the other. For it is only the whole which properly has reality, and hence the form of pure freedom relatively to anything else, the form which takes expression as time. But the moments of the whole, consciousness, self-consciousness, reason, and spirit, have, because they are moments, no existence separate from one another (p. 689).

Phenomena, then, have no particular subsistence of their own; they are only "moments" of the totality. Any apparent independence is deceiving, for, in actuality, all moments are attributes of the essence. Think of the totality as a sphere. The center point of the sphere is the essence of the totality, while any phenomenon within the totality is analogous to all possible vectors radiating from the center. An examination of any possible phenomenon along the circumference of the sphere leads back into the center, to the essence, from which all else radiates. All phenomena along the circumference of the sphere, though they may appear to be independent, are integrally linked with all other phenomena; as attributes of the essence, they are only moments in the totality.

This description is static, however, and it only has the power of describing totality synchronically. To understand how causality operates within the expressive totality, diachrony must also be understood. Diachronically, the totality is conceived of as evolving as the essence unfolds. Put another way, the essence exercises effectivity through its parts. Depending, therefore, on the particular identification of the nature of the essence, totalities may unfold in very different ways. In such a formulation, all causality is internal to the whole, that is, the nature and appearance of any phenomenon can be seen as the effect of the unfolding of the essence, an unfolding that is manifest in all attributes of the totality. Similarly, the effectivity of any phenomenon within the totality is part of that unfolding. Thus, expressive causality is a process of unfolding of an essence as manifest by the appearance of peripheral representations.

EXPRESSIVE CAUSALITY AND ANALYSIS OF THE RELATIONSHIP BETWEEN COMMUNICATION TECHNOLOGIES AND SOCIETY

Unfortunately, few people who write about communication technologies utilizing a concept of expressive causality do so with the rigor of a philosopher. Most begin with the assumption that technologies are phenomena that express some central essence of a particular social structure. Only rarely is the nature of the essence thought through very carefully in terms that could contribute to the formulation of a theory of society, of a theory of change within a particular totality, and of change between one totality and another. Thus, it is fairly commonplace for a writer to begin—at least logically—with a technology or with technology as a generic term and, working backwards, locate the essence of the society in which the technology was produced in order to explain the origins and nature of the technology. Theoretically, once the essence of a society is located, all technologies should be explicable in its terms; so a researcher should be able to work in either direction.

Although the nature of the essence varies from one scholar to another, certain themes recur with notable frequency. So, for example, it is often some idea or ideal that forms the essence of the totality within which technology arises (the problem of the origins of those ideas or ideals generally being left to philosophers).

It is useful to examine in some detail Louis Mumford's articulation of the expressive nature of technology, for Mumford's work has had considerable influence among scholars interested in the relationship between communication technologies and society. Underlying Mumford's conception of modern technology and society is the belief that the effective essence of the totality is a mechanical conception of life. Mumford (1963) begins his exposition in *Technics and Civilization* by suggesting the origin of this essence. He states that the machine, by which he means the entire technological complex, has more than one point of origin. "Our mechanical civilization," he writes, "represents the convergence of numerous habits, ideas, and modes of living, as well as technical instruments; and some of these were, in the beginning, directly opposed to the civilization they helped to create" (p. 12). Initially this statement appears to contradict the earlier assertion that underlying Mumford's analysis of technology lies the essence of a mechanical conception of life. Yet Mumford begins his analysis at a transition point between one totality and another. In explaining the *transition*, Mumford takes a largely symptomatic position. He posits a nonmechanical society out of which a mechanical one arises, although philosophically he cannot account for how it can change. Already, all of the habits, ideas, and the like, out of which the mechanical conception of life arises, are all clearly mechanical. Those phenomena that come together are things such as the desire to control time, space, and the behavior of individuals, as well as the orderly punctual life practiced in monasteries. Thus, in a sense, the mechanistic conception of life arises within a society where mechanical ideas and habits have already become the essence of the totality, and where causality is already expressive.

The essence of society that Mumford posits, with its mechanistic habits and ideas, comes together first in the monasteries. The effect is the virtually inevitable invention of the clock, an invention that epitomizes for Mumford the very essence of the new society. Mumford writes: "The monastery was the seat of regular life, and an instrument for striking the hours at intervals or for reminding the bell-ringer that it was time to strike the bells, was an almost inevitable product of this life" (p. 13). The organizing essence, and thus the origin, of the new totality really is, in Mumford's formulation, the mechanistic conception of life. The monastic ideal of regularity both produced the clock and is further enhanced by the clock. Mumford explains: "Now, the orderly punctual life that first took shape in the monasteries is not native to mankind, although by now Western peoples are so thoroughly regimented by the clock that it is 'second nature' and they look upon its observance as a fact of nature" (p. 16). The new totality, according to this pronouncement, has won out; it has captured our imaginations as well as our activities. Even though, as Mumford points out, the monastics might have been opposed to the transference from eternity as a measure of human life to the complete mechanization of our lives, they ironically helped to produce just that change. The irony is possible precisely because the mechanistic conception of life unfolds throughout the totality, not the motivations for conceiving of it that way. Over time, the mechanistic conception of life exercises effectivity until, as Mumford maintains, it is all-embracing; it achieves total infiltration.

The most representative account of the consequences of positing an ideal essence for communication technologies has been advanced by Jacques Ellul. As explained in Chapter 4, Ellul, like Mumford, posits a preindustrial pretechnological "Golden Age." The essence of the new age, the technological society, is technique. Ellul (1964), like Mumford, fails to provide an adequate explanation of the transition from the Golden Age to the technological age, and he likewise betrays recourse to a mechanistic, symptomatic position. Machines clearly have something to do with the transition, although where the machines come from is never explained: "Technique certainly began with the machine. It is quite true that all the rest developed out of mechanics; it is quite true also that without the machine the world of technique would not exist" (p. 3). Yet Ellul also suggests an essentially contradictory explanation of origins: "the machine is deeply symptomatic: it represents the ideal toward which technique strives. . . . technique transforms everything it touches into a machine" (p. 4). This latter explanation, like Mumford's explanation of already mechanical ideas and habits that come together to form the mechanical conception of life, suggests an already expressive origin of the machines.

Regardless of its ambiguous origins, technique forms the essence of the new totality: "Technique is not an isolated fact in society (as the term *technology* would lead us to believe) but is related to every other factor in the life of modern man" (p. xxvi). Actual physical machines are only a small part (or attribute) of the complex totality. A machine is "the result of a certain technique," and "its social and economic applications are made possible by other technical advances" (p. 4).

One of the vectors of technique that bears particularly heavily on the analysis of communication technologies is propaganda. In his book *Propaganda: The Formation of Men's Attitudes,* Ellul (1973) describes propaganda as itself a system of techniques or a technique. In a broad sense, propaganda involves powers of persuasion. Yet, predictably, as merely a vector of the essence (technique), propaganda can be reduced completely to that essence. Propaganda, like technique, "*is* our culture" (p. 109). It is a "general phenomenon in the modern world" (p. vix), and Ellul sets out in his analysis of it "to consider its inescapable influence in the modern world and its connection with all structures of our society" (p. xv). Propaganda is really nothing more than the persuasive attribute inherent in technique.

For Ellul, communication technologies play a crucial role in the technological age. The age is characterized by the dissolution of the small cohesive groups, such as the family and the church, and by the overall disintegration of the traditional social structure. (These, of course, are brought about in and through the unfolding of technique throughout society.) The media both serve the new communication needs of the society and help to perpetuate the isolation and fragmentation of individuals and groups within the society. These media constitute both an effect of the unfolding of the technological society and an effective force, in that "what these media do is exactly what propaganda must do in order to attain its objectives" (p. 9). Propaganda needs the mass media—even requires them.

The very structure of communication technologies, as well as their content (where they can be said to have content), is an expression of a totality dominated by technique. Centralized control of a fragmented mass of individuals characterizes a propagandized society. Individuals in their dissipated state need something to fill their empty and frustrating lives, and so they turn to the media. To succeed, the media must fill the needs of individuals while shaping the activities of these individuals to conform to the needs of the mass-ified technoindustrial state. The media, thus, tend to be both highly centralized in terms of ownership and control, but somewhat diversified in terms of product. After all, for propaganda to work, people cannot know that they are being propagandized.

MARXIST CONCEPTIONS OF EXPRESSIVE CAUSALITY

By assuming an expressive totality within which expressive causality operates, Ellul defines both the structure and content of communication technologies as expressions of some central essence. That essence, however, need not be an idea or ideal as it is, for example, in the work of Mumford and Ellul. A particularly important Marxist variant of expressive causality has come to play an increasingly determinant role in the way we look at the relationship between communication technologies and society.

Georg Lukács (see especially, 1972, 1976) is a seminal figure in this Marxist variant of expressive causality. Although Lukács's conception of expressive causality is neither consistent nor well defined, he has been tremendously influential in shaping thinking about expressive totality and the role it has played in the Marxist tradition. Consequently, his work on totality has been indirectly influential in conveying notions of expressive causality.

Lukács's conception of totality is based on the appropriation and adaptation of the Hegelian articulation of totality. Hegel posits a universal, infinite totality characterized by three stages.[1] In the first stage, there is unity between subject and object, individual and nature; but the unity is not self-conscious. In the second stage, individuals become knowing subjects, which causes them to perceive and live in oppositions. The first opposition is to nature: "first, man as knowing subject is separated from nature, which he now sees as brute fact, not expressive of some idea or purpose. Nature is thus other than mind in not exhibiting any rational necessity or expressive form" (Taylor, 1975, p. 77). Individuals thus become alienated from nature. Yet because Hegel perceives our experience as continuous—that is, that we perceive ourselves as unified—we live in contradiction and opposition; we live in dualism. The growth of our self-consciousness produces the opposition between mind and world, between the rational will and our own "nature," between individual and community, and, finally, between the totality and its parts. The essence of the Hegelian expressive totality is spirit, or *Geist:* "That which underlies and manifests itself in all reality" (Taylor, 1975, p. 87). The universe is the embodiment of the *Geist* in finite form, and all is part of a plan, or movement, toward a higher unity. This movement is the unfolding of the *Geist:* "out of original identity, opposition necessarily grows; and this opposition itself leads to a higher unity" (Taylor, 1975, p. 87). The higher unity is realized when we come to an awareness of our rational self-awareness—that is, an awareness that, for the universe to be the embodiment and expression of the *Geist,* we must be self-conscious and therefore separated from nature and such at the same

time that we are integral to it. This development is not an individualist
one, but rather the development of the awareness of individuals as species beings. The nature of this resolution is described by Charles Taylor
(1975, p. 91):

in recognizing that this is the structure of things we at the same time shift the
centre of gravity of our own identity. We see that what is most fundamental
about us is that we are vehicles of *Geist*. Hence, in achieving full insight our
science of the universe is transformed; from being knowledge that we as finite
spirits have about a world which is other than us it becomes the self-knowledge
of universal spirit of which we are the vehicles.

It is, therefore, in the negation of unity that final unity is achieved. As
Louis Althusser (1970, p. 203) has written:

The *Hegelian totality* is the alienated development of a simple unity, of a simple
principle, itself a moment of the development of the Idea: so, strictly speaking, it
is the phenomenon, the self manifestation of this simple principle which persists
in all its manifestations, and therefore even in the alienation which prepares its
restoration.

Marxists working with a Hegelian conception of totality and causality strive to turn this idealist dialectic into a materialist one. Lukács (1976)
argues that, since the development of consciousness in Hegel depends
on its ability to reflect objective reality, it is objective reality—not the
"movement of spirit in and for itself"—that determines the theoretical
and practical activity of consciousness (pp. 473–474). According to
Lukács, the growth of consciousness is determined by economic activity
or, more specifically, by the processes of capitalist commodity relations.
For Lukács, the totality is neither universal nor infinite. Rather, it is
limited to capitalism, and the essence of the totality is the commodity
structure. In *History and Class Consciousness,* Lukács (1972) asserts that
"the problem of commodities must not be considered in isolation or even
regarded as the central problem in economics, but the central, structural
problem of capitalist society in all its aspects" (p. 83). The problem is, of
course, the commodity fetish, where relations between people take on
the character of relations between objects. People and things become
reified. The image of the whole—and with it the unity of subject and
object—is destroyed. This commodity structure penetrates society "in all
its aspects . . . to remould it in its own image" (p. 85). To recapture the
image of the whole and conjoin subject and object, the proletariat must
discover the connections between the apparent form of phenomena and

their essence. In an essentially Hegelian move, this recognition necessarily involves a transcendence of reification and alienation.

MARXIST CONCEPTIONS OF EXPRESSIVE CAUSALITY AND ANALYSIS OF THE RELATIONSHIP BETWEEN COMMUNICATION TECHNOLOGIES AND SOCIETY

In a totality with a material essence, just as in a totality with an ideal essence, technology does not exercise effectivity autonomously. Since each part of the totality is merely a moment in the social process of production, it is logically impossible for technologies to display any degree of autonomy. Max Horkheimer (1972) has written that all structures, functions, services, works, or operations "emerge rather from the mode of production practiced in particular forms of society. The seeming self-sufficiency enjoyed by work processes whose course is supposedly determined by the very nature of the object corresponds to the seeming freedom of the economic subject in bourgeois society." No matter how complex, technologies, like any other aspect of the totality, cannot "but exemplify the working of an incalculable social mechanism" (p. 197). Technologies, then, will embody and express the contradictions inherent in the unfolding of commodity relations throughout the capitalist social formation.

In 1925 Lukács (1966) wrote a review of a textbook written by Bukharin. In the review Lukács attacks Bukharin's simple causal position on the relationship between technology and society. Lukács quotes Bukharin as remarking that, "Every given system of social technique *determines* human work relations as well. . . . If technique changes, the division of labour in society also changes" (p. 29). To counteract this simple causality, Lukács claims that Bukharin inverts the Marxist dialectic. Rather, the social determinants are the social productive forces; technology (or technique, since the terms are used virtually interchangeably) is a part of those forces, and its development is to be explained in terms of those forces. There is no room for any autonomous role for technology in Lukács' schema: "For if technique is not conceived as a moment of the existing mode of production, if its development is not explained by the development of the *social* forces of production (and this is what needs clarification), it is just as much a transcendent principle, set over against man, as 'nature,' climate, environment, raw materials, etc" (p. 30). Modern mechanized techniques are then "the consummation of modern capitalism, not its initial cause" (p. 31). They are the manifestation of the contradiction between the limitation of older techniques and the changing requirements of production in incipient capitalist enterprise.

Sometimes Lukács seems simply to be reversing the poles of a simple causal position, but overall he seems to be struggling with a way to talk about technology as an expressive part of the production process. In rejecting Bukharin's simple correspondence between technique and social relations, Lukács struggles against a mere reversal of the causal poles: "Nobody doubts that at every determinant stage of development of the productive forces, which determine the development of technique, technique retroactively influences the productive forces" (p. 30). Yet once we understand that the conception of totality is one in which all of its parts are expressions of the unfolding of commodity relations, the way in which the technology retroactively influences the productive forces can only be to further develop the commodity fetish by enhancing the development of capitalist manufacturing. As Lukács states, "this *reciprocal interaction* by no means surpasses the real historical and methodological primacy of the economy over technique" (p. 31). It is a "serious error," Lukács comments, to see technique "as even only mediately determinate for society" (p. 30).

The influence of this way of thinking about totality and causality can be seen in the way in which Herbert Marcuse (1941) lays the groundwork for talking about communication technologies. Marcuse's conception of causality is closest to that of Hegel's via Lukács. Marcuse explores the way in which technology, by which he means a thoroughly integrated social process, manifests developing capitalist domination. He writes: "Technology, as a mode of production, as the totality of instruments, devices and contrivances which characterize the machine age is thus at the same time a mode of organizing and perpetuating (or changing) social relationships, a manifestation of prevalent thought and behavior patterns, an instrument for control and domination" (p. 414). In search of competitive efficiency, industry builds a highly mechanized, rationalized technology. This technology enhances the concentration of economic power, which then lends further credence to the domination of rationality as a measure of relations between individuals. Technology is, for Marcuse, the vehicle of reification, and through it individuals are deprived of any individuality. They become totally subjugated to the unfolding of the principle of capitalist production. One way that the subjugation of the individual is accomplished is through the mass media, which are organized to exert domination. If one requires proof of this, Marcuse (1964, p. xvii) argues that "telling evidence can be obtained by simply looking at television or listening to the AM radio for one consecutive hour [sic] for a couple of days, not shutting off the commercials, and now and then switching the station."

VARIATIONS OF EXPRESSIVE CAUSALITY
AND ANALYSIS OF THE RELATIONSHIP BETWEEN
COMMUNICATION TECHNOLOGIES AND SOCIETY

Undoubtedly, the single most important contemporary figure to write about communication technologies utilizing a concept of expressive causality is Raymond Williams (see especially, 1965, 1973, 1975, 1977, 1979). He is important not only because he has been tremendously influential, but because his use of expressive totality and causality is somewhat unique. Williams has strongly criticized theorists who attempt to show how a particular economic or political aspect or practice dominates the rest of life because they have "characteristically involved an extreme selectivity in this demonstration of particular consequences, and an exclusion of other kinds of activity which did not bear the stamp of any such direct relation" (1979, p. 138). Williams argues that, to overcome this selectivity, we must reassess the concepts of base and superstructure, as well as the way in which the base is characterized as determining the superstructure. The base should be thought of not as an economic abstraction controlling life, but rather as the actual activities of individuals in real social and economic relations circumscribing a range of possibilities and exerting pressures. Since for Williams the most important activity a worker is involved in is the production of his or her self, it is important to view cultural production as a primary activity along with other forms of production. What is important for Williams is that these real processes of social and cultural production constitute our lived experience. Our "sense of reality" is the organized relationship of social practices, meanings, and feelings. This organization is what Williams calls totality.

Totality is characterized by a particular shared sense of experience within a given social formation. Indeed, the shared sense of experience defines a social formation. The essence of any social formation, or totality, is what Williams calls "the structure of feeling." The phrase, which is essentially coterminous with totality, social formation, and culture, is "the particular living result of all the elements in the general organization" (1965, p. 64), "meanings and values as they are actively lived and felt," or alternatively, the "affective elements of consciousness and relationships" (1977, p. 132). In an interview with the editors of *New Left Review*, Williams (1979, pp. 167–168) suggests that the structure of feeling might actually be an area of constant tension between lived experience and that which is already articulated (that which is already given in language, for example).[2] Yet in Williams' analysis of social formations, he has always given primacy to the unity of the lived experience. For example, although he has acknowledged that a structure of feeling operating in a particular formation might include the articulation of something beyond its own experience, he has stated that with respect to literary products, "The notion of a structure of feeling was designed to focus a mode of historical and social relations which was yet quite internal to the work, rather than deducible from it or supplied by some external placing or classification" (1979, p. 164).

The concept of hegemony must be included in the explication of Williams' position, for there is never one single social formation. Rather, different social formations vie for dominance, and in any one period there will be "a central system of practices, meanings and values, which we can properly call dominant and effective" (1973, p. 9). No social formation ever achieves hegemony. Rather, a continual and active process of selecting, reorganizing, adjusting, and reinterpreting lived experience renders a social formation dynamic. Williams explains that, when you analyze a particular structure of feeling, you begin by seizing first a moment by isolating the structure in time, but you are then quickly caught up in its historical development.

Even though the formation may in fact be struggling against other formations, and changing in relation to them, the tendency in this approach is ultimately to ascribe authenticity only to the unified lived experience. The way in which practices, meanings, and values are interconnected within the formation is what is paramount. As Stuart Hall (1980, 63–64) has argued, this process is not identical to the search for a Hegelian essence. The process is, however, "essentialising" in that there is a search for common "forms" that underlie and define the totality— homologous forms that connect what are only apparently differentiated areas.

Thus, while Williams' position does not preclude the possibility of thinking of causality as external to the social formation, primacy (or authenticity) is given to the way in which it operates internally. Effectivity is characterized in an essentially two-fold movement within the totality. To begin with, a social formation is made up of practices, meanings, and values that, as pointed out earlier, are dominant and effective. In and through these practices, meanings, and values, individuals act in the world with intentions, interests, or objectives. Intentions, for Williams, need not be conscious choices; rather they are more likely to appear as the "obvious" and unquestionable social relations and practices that shape the objectives. These intentions are, nonetheless, effective; that is, they have "real-world" effects. Yet the "meaningfulness" of these effects is determined by the way they are incorporated into experience, that is, the way they are connected to other practices, meanings, and values. The essence can thus change, as practices, meanings, and values are reorganized. There is, however, always an underlying form, unity, or essence of experience in which all elements are linked. Each element is an expression of that essence.

Even when considering the clash of separate social formations, causality is still "essentialised." As a formation selects and incorporates elements from other social formations, it does so in terms of the social intentions that exercise effectivity within the totality to begin with. Those incorporated elements then become part of an essentialised totality, where all causality can be explained in terms of the effectivity of that essence.

An examination of Williams' explanation of the origins of television (1975, 14–31) illustrates how causality operates within this kind of expressive totality vis-à-vis communication technologies. Although for Williams a structure of feeling and a social formation are generally class- and generation-bound, the social formation in Williams' analysis of television seems to be industrial capitalist society in general. Williams begins by positing this social formation with "known social needs, purposes and practices" within which certain kinds of technologies are sought with "certain purposes and practices already in mind" (p. 14). A social need will not automatically produce a technology, however, for the technical ability may be absent and/or, more importantly, satisfying the need may not be a priority item in the social formation. Instead, the particular, crucial "community of selected emphasis and intention" (p. 18) determines why and how a technology develops. This community links practices, meanings, and values in a structure of feeling. The particular structure of feeling that exercises effectivity in industrial capitalist society is "mobile privatisation" (p. 26). Mobile privatisation is thus the essence that exercises effectivity, through known social needs, purposes, and practices, in determining the shape of modern communication technologies.

Williams argues that the transformation of industrial production is characterized by increased mobility and the increased scale of organizations, accompanied by increased problems of communication. Ironically, just as individuals become more mobile, they become more isolated from the rest of the world as they live in their privatized homes. In response to the needs of a society both so mobile and so privatized, transport, telegraphy, photography, motion pictures, radio, and television are developed. These technologies are effects in that they are the result of that "crucial community of selected emphasis and intention." Even though these inventions may have been built on earlier inventions, which were not developed within this structure of feeling, the social formation incorporates only those technological practices, meanings, and values that can help fulfill its intentions. Yet these technologies are likewise effective, for as part of the totality they incorporate practices and intentions that enhance mobility, centralization, and privatization. Television, with its centralized production and privatized reception is merely one practice among many that reflect, enhance, and indeed constitute the structure of feeling in the capitalist formation.

Williams writes with an unusually explicit and consistent model of causality and an equally articulate notion of the totality within which it operates. It is much more common for writers to assume an expressive position without pursuing the implications of their position. The result is often an apparently simple-minded equation of a technology with some homogeneous sense of society. This is usually done by pointing to correspondences between the technology and something about the society within which the technology has emerged. That "something" is generally what the writer feels defines the society and what is thus the essence of that totality. So, for example, when Mike Cavanagh (1977, p. 15) asserts that, "The computer is the product of a particular society, and the consumer society will produce the consumer computer," he is suggesting that the design and use of a computer produced within a consumer society is expressive of the essence of that system: consumption practices.

Even when the mechanism whereby the technologies arise is considered to be extremely complex, the technologies still reflect an essence within a totality. Such is the case in the work of Langdon Winner. In *Autonomous Technology*, Winner (1977a) writes, "technology is . . . inherently pragmatic" (p. 7), for *"different ideas of social and political life entail different technologies for their realization"* (p. 325). Winner emphasizes the difficulty of locating the ideas of social and political life that are responsible for specific technological choices. The choices, not necessarily conscious, are deeply imbedded in our normative conceptions of social and political life. To explain the relationship between society and technology, then, we must understand the normative concepts which, in a very real sense, require the development of particular kinds of technologies. Winner recognizes that "The character of a society and the changes that take place in it are the product of a vast set of possible causes—climate, geography, population, religious practices, the market, political structure, and so forth" (p. 76). Yet the "character" of society, not unlike Williams's "community of selected emphasis and intention," determines the shape and nature of technology.

Initially, then, technological development is based on specific social and political ideas. In the formulation of technical systems, however, the systems themselves, as expressions of those ideas, become part of the social totality within which further technological development occurs.

Systems have their own requirements; thus future technological developments may depend largely on the demands of the technical system. Winner describes the process thus:

One can assume that each of the technologies in question—the systems of communication, energy supply, transportation, industrial production—was originally founded upon some widely accepted purpose: the accomplishment of a particular goal or the continuous supply of a product or service. But the means to the end, the system itself, requires its own means: the resources, freedom, and social power to continue its work. It needs among other things, an atmosphere of laws and regulations to facilitate rather than limit its ability to act. . . . To ignore these demands, or to leave them insufficiently fulfilled, is to attack the very foundations on which modern social order rests (p. 259).

The megatechnical system and all future technological developments are thus consequences or expressions, of the foundation (or essence) of the modern society. Though the relationship is not one of simple reflection, the effectivity exercised by the essence, through the megatechnical system, is so complete that, "technology is now a kind of conduit such that no matter which aims or purposes one decides to put in, a particular kind of product inevitably comes out" (p. 278).

Positions that utilize a conception of expressive causality represent a considerable advance over positions utilizing simple or symptomatic conceptions of causality. The strengths of the expressive positions lie in their acknowledgement that technologies arise within a social system and that they can be explained in terms of that system. Technologies are not autonomous; they are not isolated phenomena whose effectivity is unrelated to the structures within which they emerge. Though this is the position's strength, it contains the seed of its major weakness as well. By positing the social structure as a totality within which everything can be defined as the unfolding of an essence, everything can be reduced to that essence. This is the origin of the definitions of technology that diffuse it within the entire social structure, as discussed in Chapter 1. For if technologies are nothing more than the expression of some essence, it is certainly more productive to define them in terms of that essence. Thus technology (a phenomenon) becomes a broader concept, such as "technique," and as such it is viewed as variously expressive of a particular totality. By assuming, and therefore searching for, only correspondences, writers deny the possibility that a technology might embody elements that truly contradict the essence of the totality or simply express something other than the essence of that totality. If, as Williams asserts, the technologies of a mobile privatized structure of feeling were built on technical developments that were not part of that structure, are not those received structures integral parts of that totality? Yet those received structures in no way reflect the structure of feeling. The reduction of complexity in this manner to an expression of essence, or to the connectedness of experience, truly selects from technologies only those elements whose correspondence can be demonstrated, while disparate elements are not seen as part of the totality. Expressive totality draws attention only to a part of the complexity of the social totality—the part to which correspondence can be attributed.

The problem of selectivity is particularly noticeable in the difficulty that writers have in accounting for change between totalities while remaining consistent to the logic of expressive causality. As demonstrated, this problem is particularly salient when writers attempt to account for change from precapitalist or pretechnological totalities to capitalist or technological totalities, respectively. Typically, writers are compelled to dismiss any disparate elements in the rejected totality. By focusing only on those elements in the rejected totality that form the essence of the new totality, the new totality is portrayed as a phoenix miraculously rising out of the ashes of the old to start anew.

EXPRESSIVE CAUSALITY AND TECHNOLOGICAL INTERVENTION

The logic of technological intervention guided by expressive causality magnifies the position's weaknesses. In the mechanistic positions, technology is autonomous, and intervention is based on the degree to which various social forces can be marshalled to shape those effects. In the simple position, such intervention is impossible, as the effects are both inevitable and inherent in the technology itself. In the symptomatic position, it is possible to shape and direct effects for various ends; the technology is to some degree maleable. From an expressive perspective, however, the technology can be an expression only of the totality in which it arises. Since every aspect of the totality is merely a manifestation of the unfolding of the essence, the consequences (the nature of the unfolding) are very nearly inevitable as long as the essence remains the same. If one objects to the effects of a particular technology or technical system, it is useless to try to direct or shape the effects. The problem is the essence of society, not a particular technology and not the particular social uses of the technology. Even if one technology could be eliminated, others that manifest that same essence would spring up. Thus, the only effective way to intervene in the relationship between technology and society would be to alter the essence of society such that the technologies that would arise from that point on would express a different—and presumably preferable—essence.

The Luddite response that seeks to destroy the system that the technology embodies, seems to be an appropriate response from an expressive position. By destroying the system, the Luddite would eliminate the effective essence that gives rise to undesirable technologies. Ironically, however, the logic of expressive causality tends to paralyze such intervention, for it is difficult to conceive of how individuals from within the totality can escape it—let alone change it—since they are part of the homogeneous totality. Ellul, for example, characterizes society as totally dominated by technique; individuals are totally propagandized. From whence, then, can come the impetus to change the totality?

This sense of being trapped by the logic of the position is echoed throughout the work of those who think technology in an expressive relationship with the totality. As the writer becomes more committed to a concept of totality, the more likely he or she will be trapped by its logic. The only way out is some kind of transcendence, or alternatively, the almost spurious imposition of an agent of change from outside the totality. For those positions that are largely Hegelian, the search for radical self-awareness eventually leads to the resolution of subject and object, and it thereby alters our relationship to the "real" world. Technology would then reflect real relations, not alienated ones. This is initially an intellectual activity, but it is presumed to have consequences for all of life. Horkheimer (1972), presupposing the freedom (if only ultimately) of individuals from the dualism of subject and object, argues that the very understanding of the way in which we have been falsely constituted by that dualism will "demand activity and effort, an exercise of will power, in the knowing subject" (p. 230). If people can get the theory right "in their heads," they will naturally "have it there in its totality and act according to that totality" (p. 240). Technological intervention is thus not really separate from the general search for "the truth." Although Horkheimer bows, though only slightly, to the necessity to reconstruct the economy ["there is still need of a conscious reconstruction of economic relations" (p. 241)], the real transformation of society will come about "via concern for social transformation" (p. 233). That this realization of self-awareness is in fact transcendence is acknowledged by Horkheimer. "Critical thinking," he argues, "is motivated today by the effort really to transcend the tension and to abolish the opposition between the individual's purposefulness, spontaneity, and rationality, and those work-process relationships on which society is built" (p. 210).

Jacques Ellul suggests, as well, that some kind of transcendence might be possible. In addition, he suggests that outside forces might wrest change in the totality which would, by derivation, change the technology. Ellul (1964, p. xxx) has outlined three means whereby the course of history might be changed:

———

1) If a general war breaks out, and if there are any survivors, the destruction will be so enormous, and the conditions of survival so different, that a technological society will no longer exist.

2) If an increasing number of people become fully aware of the threat the technological world poses to man's personal and spiritual life, and if they determine to assert their freedom by upsetting the course of this evolution, my forecast will be invalidated.

3) If God decides to intervene, man's freedom may be saved by a change in the direction of history or in the nature of man.

Apart from those cases of *Deus ex Machina,* a notion of individual freedom runs through these prescriptions for change, but unfortunately the logic of expressive causality makes it very difficult to see just how individuals can be free in this sense within a truly consistent expressive totality.

Setting aside for the moment the logical problem of accounting for an agent of change from within a totality, consider the options for intervention provided by an expressive position. If the essence is the issue, then the essence is the only appropriate site for intervention. Symptomatic-style interventions after the fact are inappropriate as ultimately they can only be ineffective. There is nothing meaningful we can do about the technologies that we already have. Alternatively, how do we attack an essence? How would we go about eliminating, for example, something as nebulous and pervasive as mechanism? While it is true that expressive causality at least points to the social determinants of invention as crucial aspects of the relationship between technology and society, it cannot direct us to specific locations for intervention.

Given the theoretical limitations of expressive causality, intervention based on it consists largely of intellectual activity: writing, thinking, spreading the "truth," and often just plain wallowing in pessimism. Granting these theorists the benefit of the doubt, we might call them "intellectual Luddites." We are left waiting for the *Deus ex Machina.*

FOOTNOTES

[1] The summary of the nature of the Hegelian totality is based largely on Taylor (1975, 76–124).

[2] In spite of changes in Williams' position over the years, I treat him as maintaining a consistent position. On the seminal matter of experience, the changes are variations on a consistent theme. Eagleton (1978, p. 22) has written, "this insistence on experience, this passionate premium placed upon the 'lived,' . . . provides one of the centrally unifying themes of Williams's *oeuvre.*"

chapter seven

Structural Causality

The critiques of simple, symptomatic, and expressive causality suggest the need for an alternative model for understanding the effective relationship between communication technologies and society. We need a model that can account for the origins of technology and that can explain the ways in which technologies embody or manifest the social structure and values that give them birth. Mechanistic conceptions of causality cannot provide the theoretical tools for understanding technology in that way. We must also be able to consider the degree to which technologies can embody and propagate truly contradictory and conflicting social dynamics. Expressive causality, in reducing totality to a single dynamic, cannot provide the theoretical tools for considering both contradiction and correspondence. What is clearly in order, then, is an alternative model of causality.

An alternative model of causality will provide us with an alternative approach to intervention. A more compelling model of causality ought to provide us with a superior approach to intervention. Previous chapters have demonstrated that interventions based on simple, symptomatic, and expressive causality have serious shortcomings. A simple causal model leaves virtually no room to intervene at all. A symptomatic model enables us to intervene only after the appearance of technology; it gives us no justification for intervening at the level where social forces give rise to invention and innovation to begin with. Expressive causality begins to address the problems of intervention before the fact but cannot provide us with the means for determining where and how to intervene in a way that will make any difference at all. Furthermore, expressive causality strips us of any justification for intervening after the fact. An alternative approach to intervention, one that is based on a more powerful model of the relationship between technology and society, should provide us with the tools for intervening both before and after the appearance of technologies. Furthermore, it should give us some way for determining specific locations for interventions such that our interventions will make a difference.

Structural causality can provide us with just such an alternative. By conceiving of causality as structural, the atomistic and autonomous characterization of cause and effect is rejected. Similarly, the reductionist, expressive characterization of effectivity as the homology between the essence and its manifestations is denied. By contrast, *structural causality posits that causes do not exist apart from their effects and that structure, which exercises effectivity, consists of its effects.*

Structural causality is largely foreign to our way of thinking about causality, given that we tend to think in mechanistic or expressive terms. A number of writers and philosophers nevertheless have expounded theories of structural causality. For example, both Spinoza and Marx have been considered to have explained causality in structural terms, though in very different ways (Althusser & Balibar, 1977, 187–193). Given the complexity of the concept, its general tenets as they are manifest in the works of a variety of authors will not be explored. Rather, one particular theory of structural causality, developed in the discourse of Althusserian structuralism, will be explicated. The concept of structural causality, as developed by the French philosopher Louis Althusser and his colleagues and students, Etienne Balibar and Nicos Poulantzas in particular, is well suited to overcoming the limitations of simple, symptomatic, and expressive causality.

A conception of structural causality as developed within the Althussarian tradition requires a radical reformulation of the way we talk about technologies. It is no longer possible to characterize technologies as atomistic and autonomous, acting, or acted on, in a simple linear fashion. In contrast, a structural causal position posits technologies as very much a part of the social structure within which they arise and exercise effectivity. A structural causal position, however, denies that technologies are merely the peripheral expressions of some central essence or organizing principle of society. Rather, it posits technologies as having relative autonomy within a complex social formation.

Structural causality assumes society as a certain kind of "whole," or totality, but not as an expressive totality. To understand how causality operates within that whole, it is first necessary to understand the nature of the whole. In a summary statement of the nature of the social whole, Althusser (Althusser & Balibar, 1977, p. 97) maintains that:

it is a whole whose unity . . . is constituted by a certain type of *complexity*, the unity of a *structured whole* containing what can be called levels or instances which are distinct and "relatively autonomous," and co-exist within this complex structural unity, articulated with one another according to specific determinations, fixed in the last instance by the level or instance of the economy.

An explanation of this definition of totality provides a basis for understanding what is implied by structural causality.

The social whole is constituted in the relationships in and between three levels: the economic, the political, and the ideological. Building on the Marxist base–superstructure metaphor, Althusser conceptualizes these three levels as corresponding roughly to the base and superstructure. The base corresponds to the level of the economic; the superstructure corresponds to the political (which contains two instances: the political and the juridical) and the ideological (Althusser, 1971, 134). Positing a correspondence between the levels and the base–superstructure metaphor renders it easier to conceive of determination in the last instance by the economic. Too literal an interpretation of the metaphor, however, renders the effectivity of the levels within the social whole difficult to conceive. Nevertheless, there is some similarity.

As Poulantzas has pointed out, these levels are abstract concepts that can be used to characterize any social structure. The specific historical articulation of the levels, however, can be understood only when they are related to, or located within, a given mode of production. Poulantzas (1978b, p. 17) explains that:

The economic, the political and the ideological are not already constituted essences, which then enter into external relations with each other, according to the schema of base and superstructure. . . . The articulation peculiar to the totality of a mode of production governs the constitution of its regional instances.

It is not possible, therefore, to delineate in abstract terms a uniform object of study of the various levels for all modes of production, only for specific ones. The aim in defining the levels is rather to move from more abstract concepts of the levels to more concrete concepts, so that they afford access to knowledge of real, concrete historical formations. All three of these levels, however, present difficult conceptual problems, regardless of the degree to which they are abstracted.

———

The *economic*, in general, is made up of three invariant elements. These are, as extrapolated from Marx by Poulantzas (1978b, p. 26):

1. *The labourer,* the "direct producer", i.e., *labour–power*
2. *The means of production,* i.e., the *object* and the *means* of labour.
3. *The non-labourer* who appropriates to himself the surplus labour, i.e., the *product.*

The manner in which these elements combine constitutes a given mode of production. This combination, according to Poulantzas, will be composed of a relationship between relations of real appropriation (that is, the relationship of the laborer to the means of production) and the relations of property (that is, the ownership of the means of production, labor power, and product). In the combination in the capitalist mode of production, of course, the laborer is separated from the means of production both in terms of property and real appropriation. The means of production are owned by nonlaborers, who appropriate surplus value, and the laborers become an element of capital, selling their labor power as a commodity.

The level of the political is undoubtedly the most difficult to define, in both abstract and regional terms. In contemporary Marxist debate, some of the most difficult challenges in the formulation of revolutionary theory and practice arise from articulating the role of the state, the relationships between political practices and state power, politics and history, and the state and the level of the economic. The resolution of this debate deeply involves the problem of explaining what it means to talk about the political. The problem is so immense that extensive study has been devoted to the problem of the role of the state and the definition of the political (see, for example, Poulantzas, 1978b). While some resolution of the debate over the political has significant bearing on this study, it is not within the scope of this book to enter into the debate and attempt to resolve the issue. Doing so would entail—at the very least— another study. Thus, at the risk of sacrificing philosophical and theoretical rigor, the political is defined as the institutionalized power of the state, as well as political practice having as its objective state power (such as the political class struggle). The predominant political structures in capitalism are juridical and political structures (the law and the state). A problem with this formulation of the "juridico-political superstructure of the state," is, as Poulantzas (1978b, 42) points out, that the law and the state are two relatively autonomous levels in themselves. There certainly is a close relationship between them, but we must be prepared to examine not only how they are relatively autonomous, but also how they combine within a particular social formation.

The level of ideology is, of the three levels, the most carefully articulated within Althusserian discourse, though it is perhaps the most difficult to describe. *Ideology* is, stated at the most rudimentary level, "a system (with its own logic and rigour) of representations (images, myths, ideas or concepts, depending on the case) endowed with a historical existence and a role within a given society" (Althusser, 1970, p. 231). Ideology is not false consciousness, and its presence is not limited to the capitalist mode of production. Rather, ideology is a "structure essential to the historical life of societies," and *"an organic part of every social totality"* (p. 232). The way we live our lives, the way we live the relationship between ourselves and the world, the very conception of what "we" means is ideology. Ideology "naturalizes" its apparent reality; that is, it is a system of representations within which we see ourselves or live our lives in a relation to our conditions of existence. Ideology does "designate a set of existing relations," but "it does not provide us with a means of knowing them. In a particular (ideological) mode, it designates some existents, but it does not give us their essences" (p. 223).

Due to this unique role of ideology, as both designating real relations but not necessarily revealing their essences, ideology is often referred to as the "imaginary relation" between individuals and their real conditions of existence. Yet the term "imaginary" is not meant to convey falsification. A passage from Althusser (pp. 233–234) highlights this reality of the imaginary and its real role in human life:

In ideology men do indeed express, not the relation between them and their conditions of existence, but *the way* they live the relation between them and their conditions of existence: this presupposes both a real relation and an *"imaginary"*, *"lived"* relation. Ideology, then, is the expression of the relation between men and their "world", that is, the (overdetermined) unity of the real relation and the imaginary relation between them and their real conditions of existence. In ideology the real relation is inevitably invested in the imaginary relation, a relation that *expresses* a *will* (conservative, conformist, reformist or revolutionary), a hope or a nostalgia, rather than describing a reality. . . .

It is in this overdetermination of the real by the imaginary and of the imaginary by the real that ideology is *active* in principle, that it reinforces or modifies the relation between men and their conditions of existence, in the imaginary relation itself. It follows that this action can never be purely *instrumental;* the men who would use an ideology purely as a means of action, as a tool, find that they have been caught by it, implicated by it, just when they are using it and believe themselves to be absolute masters of it.

Ideology thus produces subjects; that is, it defines and shapes for us our own subjectivity. It actively constitutes our experience of ourselves and thereby our conditions of existence.

Ideology constitutes our experience in a profoundly unconscious way. So, for example, capitalism develops a juridical system to protect property rights. In our relationship with that system, a humanist ideology of individuals who are free and equal under the law emerges. The juridico-political system requires that we think ourselves, and act, as individuals who are free and equal, though such an ideology ignores the fact that it is only in that ideology that we are so constituted. Yet the ideology is an active principle in further reinforcing or modifying our conditions of existence, even when we recognize it as ideology. So, for example, when we protest the inequities in the juridical system, we are likely to protest on the grounds that it does not treat us as free and equal beings. Thus, possible reformation of the juridical system can modify our conditions of existence "in the imaginary relation itself." So not only does ideology constitute our experience, but it is also historically effective; that is, it acts as a determining force.

One additional point requires emphasis—that ideology exists in structures. Ideologies are, as Althusser (1976, p. 155) states "bodies of representations existing in institutions and practices." Ideology is not generally a conscious set of representations to which we ascribe and with which we then act in accordance. We do not, for example, consciously think of ourselves as free and equal and then construct a juridical system to reflect that. Rather, through the structure of the law, the constitution of free and equal beings is "imposed" on us.

The three levels—the economic, the political, and the ideological—as stated earlier, co-exist within a complex structural unity in which they are both relatively autonomous and determined in the last instance by the economic. The unity of the whole is, as Althusser (1970, p. 202) maintains, *"the unity of a structure articulated in dominance."* Within this structure, each level has its own logic of development and its own effectivity. Each level thus develops unevenly, not in simple correspondence to the other levels. At any given time, this structure is articulated in dominance; that is, there is a hierarchy of effectivity, and, in a particular historical formation, the different levels will have different degrees of effectivity. Thus, a revolution in the level of the economic would not necessarily automatically produce corresponding changes in the other levels. These other levels might have, in such a case, as explained by Althusser (1970, p. 116), "sufficient of their own consistency *to survive beyond their immediate life context,* even to recreate, to 'secrete' substitute conditions of existence temporarily." Determination by the economic is thus never active in a pure state. As Althusser (1970, p. 113) declares in an often quoted sentence: "in History, these instances, the superstructures, etc.—are never seen to step respectfully aside when their work is done or, when the Time comes, as his pure phenomena, to scatter before

His Majesty the Economy as he strides along the royal road of the Dialectic." The particular strength of this insight is that it is possible to explain theoretically why, in fact, the economic, the political, and the ideological often seem to contradict one another, affect one another, and evolve somewhat autonomously.

But the fact that the levels are semiautonomous does not render them independent. They are, in fact, in a certain kind of dependence with respect to the whole. The economic is, after all, determinant in the last instance. Balibar (Althusser & Balibar, 1977, p. 224) broadly defines the meaning of determination in the last instance thus: "In different structures, *the economy is determinant in that it determines which of the instances of the social structure occupies the determinant place.*" The economy therefore, in its particular regional structure, determines whether, for that mode of production, the level of the political, of the ideological, or of the economic itself plays the dominant, effective role in the structure in dominance. The *hierarchy of effectivity* of the levels is thus determined by the economic. The whole is thereby defined by the particular regional structure of the relationships between the levels. As Althusser (1970, p. 213) has stated: "in real history determination in the last instance by the economy is exercised precisely in the permutations of the principle role between [the levels]."

This complex structured whole cannot be conceived without contradiction. The uneven development of the levels compels contradiction just as the presence of the contradictions defines the whole: "every contradiction is a contradiction in a complex whole structured in dominance" (Althusser, 1970, pp. 204–205). The structure in dominance thus generates contradictions that animate and constitute the structure in dominance. Contradiction is, as must now be obvious, the motive force of all development. The principal contradiction (that is, the abstract economic contradiction between the forces and relations of production), as Anthony Giddens (1979, p. 155) has explained the process, "expresses itself through the asymmetry of the other levels within the totality." This resulting asymmetry generates secondary contradictions, contradictions that reflect *their* conditions of existence.

So, then, in any given social formation, there will be not only a principal contradiction between the forces and relations of production, but also secondary contradictions as well. The nature of these secondary contradictions will vary (both in kind and location) as determined by the particular changing configuration of the structure in dominance. These contradictions are what Althusser (1970, p. 209) calls "overdetermined," that is, they reflect their conditions of existence, their "situation in the structure in dominance of the complex whole." A contradiction is "determined by the structured complexity that assigns it to its role." Secondary contradictions are not, however, "pure" expressions of the primary or general contradiction, precisely because their conditions of existence also consist of the effectivity of the political and the ideological levels, which have their own degrees of consistency, effectivity, and autonomy. There is, then, no simple contradiction from which all else flows, but only particular overdetermined contradictions. Each overdetermined contradiction is "inseparable from the total structure of the social body in which it is found, inseparable from its formal *conditions* of existence, and even from the instances it governs; it is radically *affected by them,* determining, but also determined in one and the same movement, and determined by the various *levels* and *instances* of the social formation it animates" (Althusser, 1970, p. 101).

Because determination in the last instance by the economic merely means that the economic determines the hierarchy of effectivity of the levels, overdetermined secondary contradictions may exercise dominant historical effectivity at a particular moment or instance. It may well be, as Althusser (1970, p. 98) suggests in the assessment of a particular historical moment, that "the real contradiction was so much one with its 'circumstances' that it was only discernible, identifiable and manipulable *through them and in them.*" It may well be, as this quotation of Althusser suggests, that attempts to intervene at the site of historically specific dominant and effective secondary contradictions might be more effective than attempts to confront the largely abstract primary contradiction directly.

In sum, causality is structural in that effectivity is exercised in and through overdetermined contradictions. The primary contradiction is active in all the secondary contradictions, but, given the relative autonomy of the levels, it cannot be argued that the secondary contradictions are mere reflections of it. The particular configuration of the complex structured whole—as it is structured in dominance—will determine the locus and nature of these overdetermined contradictions. These contradictions will then affect the real conditions of existence, determining essentially the structure. Causality is, then, internal to the structure. There are no autonomous, atomistic causes or effects external to it. As Althusser (Althusser & Balibar, 1977, pp. 188–189) writes:

This implies therefore that the effects are not outside the structure, are not a pre-existing object, element or space in which the structure arrives to *imprint its mark:* on the contrary, it implies that the structure is immanent in its effect, a cause immanent in its effects in the Spinozist sense of the term, that the *whole existence of the structure,* in short that the structure, which is merely a specific combination of its peculiar elements, is nothing outside its effects.

The problem of inevitability, a problem neither the mechanistic nor expressive positions could escape entirely, is not a problem in this position. With the levels relatively autonomous, the real conditions of existence are not predetermined. The locus and nature of secondary contradictions are not absolutely given, not entirely determined by the economic. Rather, they are overdetermined by the particular way in which the semiautonomous levels generate contradiction in the complex structured whole.

Structural causality presents an alternative to the atomism of simple and symptomatic causality. Similarly, it presents an alternative to the idealist conception of expressive causality that posits all causes and effects as expressions of some inner essence or contradiction. Structural causality permits a vision of the social whole as a complex structured unity, structured in dominance, in which all cause and effect are internal to the totality, but not simply inevitable reflections of some essence. We can thus acknowledge that the various semiautonomous levels in the whole will exercise effectivity, as determined by their particular configuration in a historically constituted complex structured whole.

STRUCTURAL CAUSALITY AND CRITICAL ANALYSIS OF THE RELATIONSHIP BETWEEN COMMUNICATION TECHNOLOGIES AND SOCIETY

How does technology fit into the conception of causality as structural? How do we approach the problem of analyzing communication technologies utilizing these insights? What will appropriate technological intervention look like? It can now be made clear why, and in what sense, the argument has been made for a definition of technology as object, rather than as some totalizing conception, such as technology as a way of life or as a human activity. As definitions embody ways of seeing, an attempt to define technology serves to direct our gaze toward technology as constituted in a particular way. Seeing technology in structural terms provides us with the critical tools to understand and critique the effective relationship between technology and society. Furthermore, it provides us with a basis for critical technological intervention.

The sense in which technology is an object from a structural causal position is clearly different from that of the mechanistic positions. As pointed out earlier, technologies are not autonomous objects isolated from the social structure within which they exist. Rather, technologies are semiautonomous elements located within a specific historical configuration within a mode of production. Although a technology is thus a real object (a real machine or structure), it is at the same time part of a changing whole that is structured in dominance. A technology, then, has no essence, and it therefore cannot reflect or express an essence, as is maintained in the expressive causal position.

The constitution of technology in this way requires subjecting our conception of technology to its historical specificity. We must recognize that a technology's relationship to society, its relative autonomy, its position in the structure in dominance, and therefore its identity as both cause and effect are all subject to historical specificity. This recognition implies that it is possible for technologies, in various social formations, to display varying degrees of autonomy and to occupy positions of varying significance in the structure in dominance. It is thus no longer possible to talk about, for example, "the nature of the computer." The computer is an historical object in a particular historically constituted configuration. Assuming that the same physical object exists in a different historically constituted configuration, that same physical object might be a quite different historical object, located in entirely different relationships in the structure in dominance. It is no longer possible to generalize about "the technology" as being identically constituted in all situations or as exercising effectivity based on the expression of its essence. Technology has no essence in that sense. It is an object, granted, but one both that is an effect and that exercises effectivity only within a particular social whole.

The starting point, then, in an analysis of the relationship between communication technologies and society should not be to explain the nature of the raw material "technology." Starting any analysis by talking about the technology—as if it had an essence—is misleading. Rather we must begin by understanding how technologies have been historically constituted—the way in which, and the degree to which, the structure in dominance has overdetermined technologies as effects, as well as rendered them effective. We must strive to locate technologies within a particular historically constituted social whole and to explain the relationships between the technologies and the whole as it changes. The logic of overdetermination requires that a single element, such as a technology, be thought of as a part of that whole, which is forever changing. Ideally, an appropriate analysis of the social whole would consist of explaining how the particular structure in dominance overdetermines technological development as well as explaining the role of technology within that whole. The attempt to describe this complex relationship is, of course, confounded by the fact that the whole is continually and unevenly changing. Obviously, the ideal description is beyond the capabilities of a single researcher or a single research project. The whole is simply too complex, as are the dynamics of change within that whole, to exhaustively explicate either a particular historical moment or a particular effective relationship.

Yet to recognize this limitation is not to undercut the value of conducting analyses of technologies from a structural causal perspective. Indeed, the very knowledge of the limitations of analysis is appropriately humbling and mitigates against dogmatic pronouncements of understanding "everything." A researcher can only hope to explicate some relationship between technologies and the various levels, although hopefully the particular dynamic isolated will be an important one, that is, one that demonstrates a considerable degree of effectivity.

The analytic isolation of particular dynamics for analysis is unavoidable when one utilizes a concept of a whole or totality. Such is certainly the case even for researchers working within the expressive causal tradition. Williams (1975, 14–31), for example, focuses on the way in which television, with its home-centered reception and centralized production, reflects "mobile privatisation." Yet the difference between the nature of the isolation of dynamics in the notion of structural causality, as opposed to that in expressive causality, is that what is being sought is the ascertainment not of homology between phenomena and essence, but of particularly dominant effective relationships. The structural causal attitude, unlike any of the others discussed, is consistent with an openness to incorporating new knowledge of new relationships in and between the levels of the political, the economic, and the ideological in the gradual construction of the understanding of the complex structured whole.

The researcher thus sets about to uncover particularly dominant effective relationships. As pointed out earlier, these relationships are not necessarily simple reflections of the primary contradiction of a particular mode of production. Rather, these dominant relationships are more likely to be explained by the nature and locus of secondary contradictions within the social whole.

STRUCTURAL CAUSALITY
AND CRITICAL TECHNOLOGICAL INTERVENTION

Technological intervention is most likely to be effective at the points of particularly dominant effectivity. Just as the location of dominant effectivity can be explained only in historical specificity, particular and appropriate technological intervention can likewise be determined only in relationship to that specificity. There can be no generalized prescription for appropriate intervention in the relationship between communication technologies and society. Yet once technologies are understood as situated in particular dominant effective relationships, the particular kind and focus of intervention required to effect change will be illuminated.

Structural causality presents a real, constructive alternative to the conceptions of causality discussed earlier. Likewise, it can point the way to effective, historically specific technological intervention. Intervention built upon a conception of the structural causal relationship between communication technologies and society acknowledges that technologies are not autonomous, isolated phenomena whose effectivity is either inherent—as in simple causality—or determined solely by social forces after they arise—as in symptomatic causality. Nor are technologies merely a peripheral reflection of some essence, as in expressive causality. Rather, technologies are part of the unevenly developing complex structure in dominance that determines their effectivity. The historically specific constitution of this social whole prohibits the adoption of a single formula for intervention, such as destroying machines and/or social structures or being trapped in paralytic pessimism (as the Luddites are wont to be), developing alternative technologies (as the Alternative Technology movement proposes), or coordinating implementation of technologies to benefit particular economic interests (as Technology Assessment does). We have seen the limitations of these forms of intervention, limited as they are by deficient conceptions of the causal relationship between communication technologies and society.

This is not to say, however, that appropriate technological intervention, relative to particular historical specificity, might not include interventions that resemble those of Technology Assessment, Alternative Technology, or Luddism. It may perhaps be appropriate to destroy machines or social structures, develop alternative technologies, or adjust technological implementation vis-à-vis particular economic interests. Yet the suggested implementation of particular strategies must be relative to specific situations and not generalized, institutionalized strategies that are deemed relevant for any and all situations. The logic of structural causality, unlike the logic of simple, symptomatic, or expressive causality, requires that we reject generalized notions or laws as universally determining the precise nature of the relationship between communication technologies and society. We must instead seek the particular dominant effective relationships that define the specific relationship between communication technologies and society for historically specific moments. Once our understanding of that relationship is informed by this historical specificity, intervention based on this conceptualization is much more likely to be truly critical and truly effective.

section three

chapter eight

The Relationship Between Patent Law And the Invention and Innovation Of Communication Technologies

Arguing for the merits of structural causality on a theoretical level, as in Chapter 7, is one thing. An entirely different matter is to demonstrate that structural causality is a useful tool in analyzing the development of communication technologies and in prescribing particular technological interventions. This chapter demonstrates that, in fact, utilizing a conception of structural causality encourages a compelling understanding of the relationship between communication technologies, systems, and the social whole or formation. In addition, this understanding suggests locations for technological interventions where they can be effective in altering that relationship.

Ideally, this analysis would examine precapitalist and capitalist modes of production, the structures of dominance with each, and the changing effective relationship between the social formations and communication technologies and systems as these formations change. In an effort to limit this study to manageable proportions, the chapter examines only the relationship between patent law and the invention and innovation of communication technologies in the capitalist mode of production, with an emphasis on the way this relationship operates within the changing capitalist social formation in the United States.

There are sound practical and theoretical reasons for thus limiting the demonstration. To begin with, the limitation is based on an intuition that the development of communication technologies has been, and is, dramatically shaped by patent law. One need only read the biographies of individual inventors in communication, such as Edwin Howard

Armstrong (Lessing, 1956) and Philo T. Farnsworth (Everson, 1949) to be convinced that, at least in individual cases, patent law has had a dramatic effect on the lives of individuals and in the development of specific inventions. Similarly, one need only read accounts of the use of patents within specific communication industries, such as telephony (Danielian, 1939; Kingsbury, 1915) and broadcasting (Maclaurin, 1971) to be aware that certain industries have used patent law, in conjunction with the invention and innovation of specific kinds of technologies and technical systems, to enhance monopolization and domination of the marketplace. Yet the mere accumulation of anecdotal information—how patents either did or did not play an effective role in a specific case—is not what is sought here. What is sought is a broader understanding of the relationship between patent law and communication technologies in the changing formations in capitalism. By drawing the broader parameters, we should be able to locate the dominant effective elements in this relationship that give meaning to the anecdotal cases.

Beyond this largely intuitive justification for the particular definition of this study, there are sound theoretical reasons for believing that it may in fact be tapping a particularly dominant effective relationship in capitalism in general and, by derivation, in the development of communication technologies and systems in capitalism. In the capitalist mode of production, the level of the economic is not only determinant in the last instance, but it is also the dominant level; that is, the capitalist mode of production is preponderant in the levels of both the political and ideological. This does not mean that the political and ideological levels do not possess relative autonomy, only that the economic exercises dominant effectivity (Poulantzas, 1978b, 15–16, 29). Thus we can expect that the economic will play an effective role in the development of communication technologies and systems. Further, in the capitalist mode of production, the juridical system, as Poulantzas (1978b, p. 56) points out, is "a condition of the functioning of the economic, in that it not only fixes relations of production in the relations of formal ownership, but it also constitutes a framework of cohesion for commercial encounters, including those for the purchase and sale of labour power" (see also pp. 71–72; Marx, 1972, 3–6; Marx & Engels, 1970, 79–81). Thus we can expect that patent law—the body of law designed to create property rights in invention—might, even more directly than the economic, play a particularly effective role in the development of communication technologies and systems. It is therefore at least possible to submit at this point that the particular way in which this study is limited ought to provide a vehicle to uncover particularly dominant effective relationships between communication technologies and the social formation.

Once we understand the nature of the relationship between patent law and the invention and innovation of communication technologies, we can evaluate elements of that relationship. Are aspects of this relationship desirable? Undesirable? Should some elements be enhanced? Eliminated? Are the consequences of this relationship satisfactory? Unsatisfactory? Such evaluation is, of course, judgmental, as is all evaluation. Yet these judgments are at least based on a sound understanding of the relationship between patents and communication technologies. Although some readers may not agree with my particular evaluation of the relationship between patents and the invention and innovation of communication technologies, they will nonetheless be able to examine the analysis upon which these judgments are based and use that same analysis upon which to base alternative evaluations.

Obviously, alternative evaluations of the relationship between patents and communication technologies will suggest different interventions. The interventions proposed in this chapter are designed to eliminate what the author views as undesirable aspects of that relationship. Proposing particular interventions demonstrates the way in which a structural causal understanding points to specific locations for intervention, given the particular evaluation. Also demonstrated is how these interventions, based on a structural understanding, are likely to be effective—that is, how they are likely to accomplish in practice what they are designed to accomplish in theory. The obvious reason for this demonstration is that a structural causal perspective should provide superior understanding upon which to base judgment and to build strategies for intervention.

This chapter delineates the effective relationship between communication technologies, technical systems, and patent law as it proceeds through three stages. The first stage corresponds roughly with the early development of capitalist relations of production. In this stage, the development of patent law arises alongside the growth of speculative investment in capital-intensive, competitive enterprise, and it encourages the development of technologies and systems that are shaped by the incipient capitalist mode of production and that contribute to its growth. In the second stage, technologies are developed that, in conjunction with patent law, are used as tools to insure the domination of particular institutions in competition with the interests of other institutions or individuals. These two stages are not strictly sequential, and indeed they exist to some degree coterminously. There is, however, a shift in the hierarchy of effectivity of the elements from the first to the second stage, a shift that accompanies the development of late capitalism. The delineation of stages is meant only to draw attention to this changing hierarchy of effectivity. The third stage is the one that we may now be entering. Though it too involves a particular configuration of the effective elements of the first two stages, a new and particularly important element is added to the matrix of determination. In this stage, patent law becomes the site of increasingly intense battles to extend patent protection to new forms of ideas embodied in modern developments, such as computer software. In this third stage, attention is directed to a crucial conjuncture where technological intervention might be effective.

THE EARLY DEVELOPMENT OF THE RELATIONSHIP BETWEEN PATENT LAW AND THE INVENTION AND INNOVATION OF COMMUNICATION TECHNOLOGIES AND SYSTEMS

A patent issued in the United States confers the right to exclude others from making, using, or selling a particular invention. A monopoly—the exclusive control of a commodity or service within a given market—is thereby conferred by the granting of a patent. A patent grant confers this virtual monopoly for seventeen years from the date of issue, during which time the patentee can prohibit the use of the same invention even if it is developed independently. Upon issue of the patent, the invention is made public through publication of a description in the United States Patent Office *Official Gazette*. A copy of the patent is also made available for examination at the Patent Office and at other patent depositories throughout the country. After seventeen years, the invention becomes public property. If rights are infringed, it is the responsibility of the patentee to institute litigation, and protection is lost only if litigation is unsuccessful (*United States Patent Law of 1952*, sec. 154). While this definition of the patent grant is, strictly speaking, accurate, it reveals little about the matrix of effectivity involved in the practice of granting patents. By tracing the historical evolution of the patent system, the effective elements of the social formation that are relevant to the relationship between the patent grant and the invention and innovation of communication technologies will be revealed.

American patent law has evolved from Venetian patent law, which was developed in the fifteenth century and spread, in variations, throughout Europe and England in the fifteenth, sixteenth, and seventeenth centuries. All these variations, including the American law, involve the same effective elements that were codified in Venetian law, although the elements exist in different effective relationships in changing social formations. Yet, because the Venetian law established effective relationships that remain effective throughout the second and third stages, it is instructive to trace the development of patent law from its beginnings in Venice. The first patent statute was passed in Venice in the early fifteenth century. There is some uncertainty regarding the date of this statute, which was apparently extended only to the silk industry (Prager, 1952, 111–112). In 1474, however, the Venetian patent system was reorganized, and a copy of that statute is extant. The text of the 1474 statute clearly reflects both an idea of inherent property rights in invention and the legitimacy of granting limited-time, exclusive monopoly rights. This statute is the model for modern European and American patent statutes, as well as for international patent standards. The relevant section of the statute reads:

> every person who shall build any new and ingenious device in this City, not previously made in our Commonwealth, shall give notice of it to the office of our General Welfare Board when it has been reduced to perfection so that it can be used and operated. It being forbidden to every other person in any of our territories and towns to make any further device conforming with and similar to said one, without the consent and license of the author, for the term of 10 years (Mandich, 1948, p. 177).

However, this statute does not merely spring from the forehead of Zeus; it is rather the overdetermined effect of the ensemble of social relations in fifteenth-century Venice. Placing the statute within this social formation provides some essential clues for understanding the changing relationship between patent law and the invention and innovation of communication technologies in the capitalist mode of production.

The economic level seems to dominate in the formulation of the Venetian statute, but some essential contributions are made by the levels of the political and the ideological in conjuncture with the economic. On the level of the economic, the Venetian patent statute was a response to changing modes and relations of production. During the fifteenth century, Italy was becoming a trading center of considerable significance, and it was beginning to develop capital-intensive industry. Weaving in particular was a dominant industry in Italy, and, during the fifteenth century, weaving centers such as Genoa and Florence became the foremost silk-weaving centers of trade in the Western world (Prager, 1952, 127–128).[1] Silk weavers had long since discovered that, by developing improved weaving techniques like water-powered twisting mills, they could produce more at a faster rate and thus gain a competitive edge on less mechanized mills. By the fifteenth century, in search of greater revenues and a competitive edge, elaborate weaving mills were being constructed, and larger and more refined weaving patterns were being designed. The production of these weavings required heavy investment for basic layouts, instruction schedules, and the building of the looms. The weaving guilds sought protection for their private speculative investment, and the 1474 Venetian patent statute was in part the result of their efforts.

The Venetian statute creates formal, legal relations of property in invention. These property relations, which protect private investment in capital-intensive industry, are immanent in the incipient capitalist mode of production. Yet these juridical relations are not purely economic relations. Juridical relations presuppose political relations—in this case, a state. In Venice the state, acting with a degree of autonomy and performing a largely cohesive function, brought together in law, semi-autonomous economic, political, and ideological factors. In particular, the early development of patent law is overdetermined by the conjuncture of the economic with the largely ideological conception of inherent rights in ideas—which is eventually identified with the notion of intellectual property—and the political practice of granting privileges.

The development of the conception of inherent rights and the practice of granting privileges are intertwined. Legal scholar Frank D. Prager, in exploring the history of intellectual property, situated its origin in the practice of granting prizes and awards for useful inventions in Persia, China, and Greece in the fourth century BC. Prizes and awards gradually became monopoly grants that conferred on the inventor the status of sole supplier of the invention or material for the government. Others were free to produce the invention or material for other sources. After monopolies were proclaimed illegal in Imperial Rome under Emperor Zeno in the fifth century AD, the creation of monopolies required convincing justification to warrant the award. Under Zeno's law, grants of monopoly to individuals were unusual. State monopolies, guild trade monopolies, contractual monopolies between individuals, and rights of property owners to their real estate and worldly goods were the predominant forms of monopoly to survive.

During the Middle Ages the practice of granting privileges appeared in more advanced industrial centers, such as Venice and Saxony. Privileges provide a key link between simple monopoly rights and patent rights. Privileges, as Prager points out, were designed to promote the useful arts and originated within circles of artisans, not within governmental bodies. The first privileges guaranteed asylum to foreign persons skilled in useful arts. While guilds generally excluded foreigners from actively pursuing their crafts, the granting of privileges assured foreign craftsmen the right to pursue certain specified crafts. These rights were granted when the contribution made by the practice of the craft was expected to benefit the particular locality where the privilege was to be exercised without damaging existing guild monopolies. Gradually these privileges acquired exclusive features and became, as Prager refers to them, "quasi-patents." Quasi-patents conveyed exclusive local rights to introduce and/or to operate specific industries. For example, the introduction of papermaking was protected in Nuremberg in 1398 when the Duke of Saxony issued a quasi-patent that was given to craftsmen who

have newly started building a paper mill downstream of the monastery at Chemnitz . . . We have given them a particular favor and grace, and let it be known by these letters that henceforth we shall not and will not allow or permit the building or making of any other or new mill, upstream or downstream or elsewhere in our country, which would or might be damaging to this mill in any manner, so long as this mill is workable and working (quoted in Prager, 1952, pp. 123–124).

The evolution of privileges and quasi-patents accompanied the growth of industries that required considerable investment in building and labor such as papermaking, mining, and smelting. These rights were clearly designed to encourage importation of useful foreign ideas as well as to encourage innovation within particular localities.

The emergence of a general practice of granting exclusive rights in invention to individuals, along with the correlative doctrine of intellectual property, was overdetermined only when a developing concept of inherent rights became an effective part of this matrix. Possibly, the sentiment that produced the doctrine of intellectual property extended further back in history than fifteenth-century Italy. Yet the doctrine first emerged there as part of an effective conjuncture in guild and government provisos, with inventors and authors claiming inherent and exclusive rights in their inventions and literary works. The first guild regulations that isolated a notion of inherent property rights appeared in 1432 in the general articles of the Genoa silk manufacturers' guild. The articles decreed that the creation of a new design gave rise to an exclusive right in that design. In 1474, the Florentine woolen guild forbade the stealing of designs from those who by their own efforts originated them. Yet as inherent and exclusive rights, they could never expire, nor could their "ownership" be transferable. Display or publication of the invention or work could in no way alter the rights of the inventor or author. A contradiction between inherent rights and privileges results, for an inherent, exclusive, and permanent right cannot be granted when and to whom the state desires in the form of a monopoly privilege. Patent law binds these two with the concept of intellectual property by recognizing inherent rights (in granting property rights) and by asserting the role of the state in promoting desired development (in granting these monopoly rights on a limited basis only).

The contradictions between economic motives, inherent rights, and the role of the state persist in all patent laws, since the fifteenth century onward, but in various social formations, certain of the elements are more dominant than others. In Venice, for example, the patent statute primarily encouraged and protected private investment in capital-intensive industry and thus leaned toward the grant as a privilege and a response to the demands to protect speculative investment. Only gradually and unevenly did the notion of inventors' inherent rights become an effective enough element in the matrix that patents were granted only to someone deemed the discoverer of an invention. For some time, just which individuals could claim property rights and concomitantly what constituted an inventor were not clear issues. Property rights were variously extended to original inventors, importers, developers, and the like. This is hardly surprising considering the effectivity of the political, in that an important aspect of granting privileges was the perception of benefit to a locality, rather than simply rewarding the act of creation or recognizing inherent rights.

This uneven development of the control of property is characteristic of the transition from precapitalist modes of production to the capitalist mode of production. The capitalist mode, as stated in the previous chapter, is characterized by a homology between relations of property and relations of real appropriation. The laborer is separated from direct ownership of the means of production, labor power, and the product (a relation of property), as well as from what is often referred to as the natural conditions of labor, as in heavy industry (a relation of appropriation). In the period of transition to the capitalist mode of production, there is a noncorrespondence between these relations, and capitalist relations of property exist before capitalist relations of appropriation. In other words, the juridical form of property exists before the capitalist is the organizer of production (Althusser & Balibar, 1977, 212–216; Poulantzas, 1978b, 157–161).

This dislocation and the gradual development of homology are manifest in the development of patent law, in the transition from protecting property rights in inventions and innovations to the gradual protection of someone deemed the original inventor. The earliest patent laws tended to protect the property rights of entrepreneurs, and they were only gradually extended to acknowledge inherent rights of an actual, original inventor. So, for example, one of the earliest patents to be issued under Venetian law was probably not granted to an inventor at all. Interestingly, this patent granted a five-year monopoly on printing in Venice to John of Speyer. In addition to the grant of monopoly on printing, it prohibited the importation of books printed outside Venice. The evidence indicates that John of Speyer might not have invented the printing press that formed the basis for his patent but probably brought the technology with him from Germany (Brown, 1891, 6–8). As this example illustrates, the law is more clearly directed toward promoting capitalistic industrial development than it is to recognizing inherent rights. Only gradually in the evolution of patent law in Europe and the United States was the issue of a patent restricted to some notion of original inventor. As this happens, it is possible for the capitalist to extend control over invention from relations of property to relations of appropriation. As patent laws are developed that acknowledge the inherent rights of an actual inventor, the relationship between the creator and his or her own subjectivity (in the act of invention) becomes potentially a capitalist one. With the new proviso—the condition of labor—the very act of invention becomes property. This makes it possible for, and encourages, capitalists to employ inventors as laborers (in a capitalist relation of property) and to direct the inventive activities of the laborers (in a capitalist relation of appropriation). Thus it is possible for the practice of invention to be largely subsumed by the double relationship between capitalist relations of property and appropriation.

The development of the relationship between patent laws and the act of invention is, of course, uneven, and, as patent laws spread throughout Europe and America, their characters are overdetermined vis-à-vis the structure in dominance of particular social formations. The effective elements remain much the same, but their effectivity varies. Thus, each configuration involves a particular conjuncture of the economic desire to protect capitalist speculative investment, the ideological belief in inherent property rights, and the political practice of granting monopoly privileges. Now added to the matrix, on the level of the political and juridical, is the effectivity of the Venetian law itself, which as stated earlier, became the model for virtually all subsequent patent systems. In large part, this was due to the demands of Venetian artisans who migrated to other European countries as Venice declined and the center of productivity shifted to other European countries (Prager, 1944, 720).

The patent system was quickly incorporated by mercantile economic formations. By developing a patent system, mercantilist states sought to encourage foreigners to immigrate and develop new technologies. Using a patent system, mercantilist states could also circumvent the control by guild monopolies, support desirable industry, and deny support to undesirable industry. In France, where the greatest degree of inherent rights in invention was reached, property rights were nevertheless limited by social obligations and subject to interference by the government. Patents were generally granted only if commercial success and/or utility could be demonstrated (Prager, 1944, 726–727). In England, where the granting of special privileges flourished during the Middle Ages, a patent policy that granted patents to inventors was initiated in 1561 (Federico, 1929b, 297). This policy accompanied and enhanced the rise of a capitalist middle class and speculative investment. The Crown's abuse of the right to grant patents is legendary, and not until 1624 was the Statute of Monopolies enacted, recognizing what was already accepted in common law: that the validity of all grants should be determined by common law. Legally, patents could thenceforth be granted only to actual inventors. Yet as legal scholar P. J. Federico (1929b, p. 303) points out, even after the passage of the Statute of Monopolies, patents were not to be granted that were "contrary to the law [or] mischievous to the state, by raising prices of commodities at home, or hurt of trade, or generally inconvenient." As a consequence, the English inventor remained considerably a petitioner of favor.

While the English Statute of Monopolies is, strictly speaking, the model for American patent law, there are some important differences in American law. As in Venice and in mercantilist Europe and England, the individual colonies in Colonial America developed a variety of ways to encourage and protect industrial development. These included the granting of bounties, premiums, subsidies, and monopolies. Fundamentally, these practices were designed not to recognize inherent rights in new inventions, but rather to encourage importation and development of manufacture from abroad, as well as to regulate existing manufacturing (Federico, 1929a; Prager, 1944, 737–739; Vaughan, 1956, 15–18). Members of colonial governments, sensitive to the abuses of monopoly that prompted the Statute of Monopolies in England in 1624, sought to temper the effects of monopoly. They were not, however, categorically opposed to monopoly. They were opposed only to monopolies that were perceived as being detrimental to the economic well-being of the colony. They tended to be highly suspicious of monopoly, but, following an essentially mercantilist drive to develop and protect industry, their policies indicate that they believed that invention and its development were useful but that its protection as property should be based on the needs of the state. Thus, for example, a statute in Massachusetts law stipulated that, "No monopolies shall be granted or allowed amongst us, but of such new Inventions that are profitable to the Countrie, and that for a short time" (quoted in Vaughan, 1956, p. 16). The granting of property rights was therefore highly dependent on the belief that such monopoly was ultimately beneficial to the economy of the particular colony. The Articles of Confederation of 1781 condoned the practice of individual states implementing their own patent policies.

In 1789 the United States Constitution (art. 1, sec. 8, cl. 8) paved the way to a unified patent policy by deeming that, "The Congress shall have the power . . . to promote the progress of science and useful arts, by securing for limited times to authors and inventors the exclusive right to their respective writings and discoveries." Nobody is really certain of the original meaning of this clause, as has been the case with so many of the

Constitution's provisions. Yet by comparing the suggested clauses with the one finally adopted, the clause evidently refers to patents and copyrights and puts them on an equal footing (Fenning, 1929, 109–117). The patent and copyright clause—as it is commonly referred to—emphasizes the power of Congress to secure exclusive rights rather than an obligation to recognize inherent rights. As a result, the particular American configuration of the relationship between the granting of monopoly favors and the recognition of inherent rights leans heavily toward the patent grant as a monopoly favor.

However, American law has developed such that an inventor is seen as having a legal right to a patent, except in cases where the granting of a patent is deemed to be "detrimental to the national security." (*United States Patent Law of 1952*, sec. 181) This legal right is extended in the belief that the country will benefit from such a right. James Madison advanced this explanation of the role of the patent and copyright clause in a discussion of the class of "miscellaneous powers" in *The Federalist*. He stated that "the utility of this power will scarcely be questioned. The Copyright of authors has been solemnly adjudged in Great Britain, to be a right at common law. The right to useful inventions seems with equal reason to belong to the inventors. The public good fully coincides in both cases with the claims of individuals" (Hamilton et al., 1852, p. 199). Based on the authority vested in it in the constitutional provision, Congress passed the first patent act in 1790. This act granted to the "petitioner or petitioners, his, her, or their heirs, administrators, or assigns, for any term not exceeding fourteen years, the sole and exclusive right and liberty of making, constructing, using, and vending to others to be used, the said invention or discovery" (quoted in, Federico, 1932, p. 250).[2] Eventually this positive right was transformed into a negative right. The Patent Act of 1952 grants "to the patentee, his heirs or assigns, for the term of seventeen years . . . the right to exclude others from making, using, or selling the invention throughout the United States" (*United States Patent Law of 1952*, sec. 154).[3] There are, therefore, two salient differences between English and American patent law: First, the English inventor is more a petitioner of favor, while the American inventor has a legal right to a patent. Second, the English right is a positive one, while the American right is a negative one.

More important than their subtle differences, however, are the similarities between American and English law. This history of American patent law indicates that we have adopted, with only slight variation, the essential tenets of the mercantilist adaptation of patent laws that grew out of the Venetian law and that spread throughout Europe and England in the fifteenth, sixteenth, and seventeenth centuries. As legal scholar S. Chesterfield Oppenheim (1951, p. 555) argued in 1951:

———

The United States has staked its national destiny and welfare upon the basic principle that private initiative, creative talents and venture capitalism shall be the primary means of determining the recipients of rewards for competitive enterprise. The American Patent System is deeply embedded in that tradition. The Constitutional provision and the laws relating to patent rights give the patentee a limited-time exclusiveness. This temporary protection against free competition is awarded in the faith that it will serve the public interest. The stated objective is to promote progress of science and the industrial arts. The exclusiveness of patent rights is regarded as a short-term public welfare monopoly which promotes the competitive economy of which the Patent System is itself a vital part.

In addition to patent law being overdetermined by the ensemble of social relations, the law itself exercises effectivity within that ensemble. In particular, a number of overdetermined effects involve the development of communication technologies that result from the conjuncture of patent law, ideology, and the economic during this stage of development. Probably the most effective conjuncture is that between patent law and ideology. As already noted, the changing labor process and the development of patent laws are characterized first by capitalist relations of property and then by both capitalist relations of property and appropriation. So not only are inventions and inventors subsumed in capitalist relations of property, but so too is the very act of invention subsumed in capitalist relations of appropriation.

Under capitalist law, persons are constituted as isolated individuals who are free and equal. They share equal rights to own property and sell their labor power. More specifically, they have the right to "own" certain ideas, which can qualify as inventions, and the right to own and organize the labor power of inventors. Nobody has any more legal right to the protection of ideas or inventions than anyone else, but individuals are equally free under the law to sell or give away their ideas and inventions as well as their inventive practice. As people act in accordance with the legal strictures to buy, sell, or protect property rights in their inventions or inventive practices, they live the humanist ideology of isolated individuals who are free and equal, as well as the ideology of the individual's right to own inventions. The ideology is so pervasive that it is difficult to see that property rights in invention are only rights created by the law, and, until a patent is obtained, there are really no rights at all. Yet the ideology is so powerful that we typically live the belief in inherent rights in our ideas. The effect of this is that we come to think of and treat technologies and the process of inventing them in that ideology; we live in part as subjects constituted by the juridical level.

The most obvious manifestation of this ideology is that invention becomes the purview of a single inventor. Since patents are ideally awarded to what is deemed the original and first inventor (*United States Patent Law of 1952,* sec. 115), any invention is seen as the product of one person's act of discovery and the property of that person. Scholarship in communication is replete with attribution of invention to a single inventor. So, for example, according to a widely used textbook in mass communication, Thomas Edison invented the phonograph, Guglielmo Marconi the radio, and Lee DeForest sound-on-film (Bittner, 1980, 207–210, 96–98, 177). Similarly, within an ideological position, researchers often criticize the attribution of inventor to particular individuals. So, for example, Gordon Hendricks (1961) argues that the "real" inventor of the motion picture was not Edison, but an employee of Edison's, W. K. L. Dickson. There are those who argue that invention ought to be thought of as some sort of group process, a social growth that, for example, "adheres to certain fairly definite patterns of impersonal causation." (Kahn, 1940, p. 480; see also, Vaitsos, 1972, p. 88–89)

This last approach is not dominant. Rather, the dominant ideology, the truly effective ideology, is that which attributes invention to individuals. Even the more enlightened communication theorists still tend to write about technologies within the dominant ideology, in that an invention is viewed as the gradual coming-together of isolated acts of invention. These isolated acts of invention eventually contribute to the construction of the invention as we know it. Harry Geduld (1975, 71–102) depicts the evolution of sound-on-film, for example, as an evolutionary process whereby various inventions accrue such that the final character of the medium consists of the conglomeration of individual inventive contributions.

This isolation of a concept of a single inventor as the creator of a single invention has not always exercised the dominant effective role that it does with the evolution of patent law and the capitalist mode of production. In a study that explodes the myth that Hans Gutenberg was the first and original inventor of printing in Europe, Pierce Butler (1940, 88–110) found that the same term, translated as "inventor," was used during the fifteenth century to refer to the discoverer of an art as well as a practitioner of an art. The crystalization of the meaning of inventor as first and original discoverer occurs as the value of printing became apparent and the construction and operation of presses required considerable investment. Butler (1940, 88–136) examines legal and personal documents that involve contractual arrangements concerning investments in printing processes and the sale and/or exchange of inventions in print technology. Clearly, as commercial relations and commercial law became more Romanized, as Butler (124–126) suggests

———

was probably happening in Germany in the fifteenth century, the at-tribution of invention to a single original inventor is overdetermined.

The inventor as a subject constituted in ideology is well suited to the reproduction of capitalist relations of production. As a laborer with inventions and perhaps even inventive practice for sale, the laborer is subjugated in capitalist relations of exploitation by the capitalist class. Yet because inventors are ideologically constituted in patent law as free and equal owners of property rights in invention and their own in-ventive labor, the inventor is denied the identification of the class nature of the capital–labor relationship.

Not only is the inventor as a subject well suited to the reproduction of capitalist relations of production, but so too is the ideological constitu-tion of invention. If invention is the purview of single individuals whose relationship to inventions is a capitalistic relationship of property and appropriation, then it is possible for capitalists to monopolize control over technologies as well. Rights to inventions can be claimed, and in so doing they can form the basis for capitalist relations of production, both as a means of acquiring surplus product and, in conjunction with the subjugation of labor, the means whereby class domination is mobilized.

In the conjuncture between capitalist economic relations, patent law, and the ideological constitution of invention and inventors, the development of communication technologies and systems are according-ly overdetermined. Communication technologies, like any other technol-ogies, tend to become, as property in capitalist relations of production, controlled by monopoly capital. In fact, the control of an invention through ownership of patent rights forms the basis of a number of monopolies in communication. This was the case, for example, with John of Speyer's patent on printing in Venice, as well as for Alexander Graham Bell's early patents on telephony, which formed the foundation of the Bell Telephone Company (Danielian, 1939, 39–44), and for Guglielmo Marconi's Radio Patents, which formed the foundation of the Radio Corporation of America (RCA) (Danielian, 1939, 107–108). Whether or not patent rights to a single invention form the basis for the establishment of a single monopoly, it is true that inventions in commu-nication are dominated by the interests of monopoly capital, and one mechanism whereby such domination is asserted is the acquisition of property rights in invention through patent law.

Yet just as important as the fact that patent law is used in conjunc-tion with the invention of communication technologies to establish mo-nopoly control over the means of communication is the fact that the communication technologies are then used by those monopolies to ap-propriate surplus value. Thus, it is evident that technologies and systems will be designed in such a way to dominate and control a particular

———

market and/or to maximize profit. The obvious result of this is the preponderant design of communication systems in which production is highly centralized, in which the product is designed to appeal to a particular market, and in which the audience is a consumer either by purchasing a commodity (as in purchasing a television receiver or a magazine), a service (as in subscribing to telephone service), or the privilege to attend a particular event (as in the purchase of a ticket to view a film). In the case where advertising subsidizes the production of the communication, the consumer pays for the commodity, service, or privilege indirectly as well through the purchase of other commodities, services, or privileges. The technologies and systems of communication are then designed to attract consumers not just of a particular communication system but of other commodities as well. Thus, for example, the television industry is built on the willingness of people to purchase television receivers as well as their willingness to purchase the products advertised on television. Profit is to be made not only in the production of television receivers, but also in the production of content for television that will attract the kinds of audiences for which advertisers are willing to pay.

Not only are individuals relegated to the status of consumers, but they are also reduced to the status of laborer in class relations. Monopoly capital in communication employs laborers to work in the production of goods and services. These laborers, as both workers and inventors, are thus subsumed in capitalist relations of class domination.

The effective relationship between patent law and the invention and innovation of communication technologies in this first stage serves to shape communication technologies and systems in such a way that they serve the interests of capital. Two aspects of this relationship are undesirable. First, because communication technologies are developed primarily to serve capital, they are not designed and shaped in response to a critical assessment of communication needs or of social, political, and economic goals. Second, communication technologies and systems are shaped uncritically in conformance to the juridico-ideological constitution of inventions, inventors, and the act of invention that suits the needs of capitalist economic production. Consequently, labor, the means of communicating, communication situations, and invention and innovation in communications are subjugated in capitalist relations of domination.

LATER DEVELOPMENT OF THE RELATIONSHIP BETWEEN PATENT LAW AND THE INVENTION AND INNOVATION OF COMMUNICATION TECHNOLOGIES AND SYSTEMS

The effectivity of the relationship between patent law and the invention and innovation of communication technologies and systems, as already described, remains much the same in the second stage, which accompanies the development of late or monopoly capitalism. In the second stage, added to the matrix of determination is the increasingly dominant role played by the competition between individual capitalists, between capitalists in one branch of industry and another, between capitalists and noncapitalists, and between owners of private property and wage earners as inventors and other laborers. The juridico-ideological structures established in the first stage serve to conceal the fact that these relations are class relations. Instead, by constituting individuals as free and equal under the law, individuals are fragmented and isolated, and relations are conceived of and lived in terms of competition, not in terms of the structural relations of a class society.[4]

Patent law in this stage is used as a tool in the competitive practices of monopoly capital. Yet the law is not strictly an instrument of the capitalist class—capitalists use it against one another as well as against noncapitalists. Rather it reflects the fact that the social formation is divided into classes in such a way that relations are conceived of and lived in competitive terms. Indeed, the most widely documented use of patent law as a tool in this stage is its use in the competitive practices between individual capitalists and between capitalists in one branch of industry and another. These practices have had considerable effect on the development of communication technologies and systems.

Industry in general has long understood the ways in which patents on inventions could be used as tools to dominate not just individual inventions but entire segments of the market. Edwin J. Prindle (1906), mechanical engineer and patent lawyer, wrote for *The Engineering Magazine* in 1906:

Patents are the best and most effective means of controlling competition. They occasionally give absolute command of the market, enabling their owner to name the price without regard to cost of production, as for example where they cover all known forms of devices for accomplishing a given purpose. There are a number of great companies whose position commercially is, or has been, due almost wholly to the possession of controlling patents (p. 809).

One of the companies he points to as having successfully utilized patents in this way is the Bell Telephone Company, which "was able to control the situation absolutely for many years, and to get itself so well located that it now has a practical monopoly in many cities, because of its being the first to occupy the field" (p. 809).

The use of patent law to control competition and to insure the survival, growth, and profitability of monopoly capital has been recognized and often criticized by countless scholars and governmental bodies throughout the twentieth century.[5] To achieve the greatest advantage over competition, patents are used to extend monopolies beyond the life of the initial patents that form the basis of the monopoly, as well as to broaden the scope of the monopoly beyond the confines of a single invention. Likewise, rapid and thorough domination of a market under patent protection renders it less likely that competitors will be able to make any inroads after the expiration of the patent monopoly.

Fritz Machlup (U.S. Congress, 1958b), in a study undertaken for the Senate Subcommittee on Patents, Trademarks, and Copyrights in 1958, described a number of tactics whereby monopoly control is extended in time and scope.[6] There are several ways to extend the life of the monopoly in the process of applying for patent protection. Because a patent runs for seventeen years from the date of issue and not the date of application, it can be beneficial to hold up the issue of the patent. Extended interference proceedings and litigation serve this purpose. Alternately, if a firm feels confident that it can keep an invention secret for a time, the actual date of application can be held up. Even the application can be constructed so that the disclosure of the invention provides information that is inadequate as a basis for replicating the invention, even after the patent expires. The act of inadequate disclosure has been elevated to an art in corporate patent practices, because the explicit purpose of disclosure is to make the idea available to the public. The Patent Act of 1952 states that the disclosure shall "enable any person skilled in the art to which it pertains, or with which it is most nearly connected, to make and use the same, and shall set forth the best mode contemplated by the inventor of carrying out his invention" (*United States Patent Law*, sec. 112). Thus inadequate disclosure must be done carefully to meet the requirements for a valid patent. Corporations also employ tactics that will extend the life of the monopoly after a patent has expired. By associating the invention with a trademark, consumer loyalty can be established that may extend beyond the patent's expiration. Contractual agreements with licensees that extend beyond the date of expiration facilitate monopoly control over time by maintaining a dominant position against possible competition. Lastly, the life of the monopoly can be extended by strategically patenting improvements on the basic patent that render the basic patent outdated.

The extension of the scope of monopoly control is often accomplished by having "basic," "umbrella," or "bottleneck" patents. A basic patent—a patent on a significant and basic invention—can act to limit the entrance of competitors at almost all levels. Bell's 1877 telephone patent is an example. An umbrella patent is one that is so broad that entrance is prohibited. An umbrella patent generally refers to a patent that would be deemed illegally broad if it were tested in court. A bottleneck patent, though not on a basic invention, is significant enough to hold up entrance into the field at a certain strategic point. Licensing agreements too can be useful in extending control over the market. Licensing agreements routinely contain restrictive provisos that demand discriminatory royalties and that dictate terms regarding products to be manufactured, quantities and levels of production, and territorial limits on markets. Often, accompanying license agreements are tie-in clauses that extend control over products not covered by the actual patent. Patent pooling or cross-licensing with other firms can function to increase the domination of those firms at the expense of competitors. Sometimes patents are simply held and not worked. As a result, an invention can be suppressed, and control is exercised by keeping everyone out of the market. This might be a useful tactic when the corporation holding the patent is producing a product with which the suppressed invention would compete. Finally, corporations routinely attempt to secure large numbers of patents, often with no intention of ever using them. Yet by controlling a broad range of patents, corporations can protect themselves from competitors who might try to "invent around" the corporation's inventions. Likewise, broad control might prohibit the entrance of possible competitors into fields nobody really anticipated would be important.

Since the 1920s, the corporate exploitation of patents has become highly rationalized. Nowhere has this been more evident than in the communication industries. American Telephone and Telegraph (AT&T) in particular is often held up as an example of a corporation that has very nearly perfected the use and abuse of patents in corporate competitive practices. Quite a lot has been written about the patent practices of AT&T and the patent battles, pooling, and licensing arrangements between AT&T, General Electric (GE), RCA, Westinghouse, and others, including nonmonpoly interests, in the 1920s (Danielian, 1939, 97–172; Noble, 1979, 87–101; Vaughan, 1956, 73–75). The 1939 report of the Federal Communication Commission's (FCC) investigation of the telephone industry includes an entire chapter devoted to the use of patent practices to build and protect the Bell System monopoly (U.S. Federal Communications Commission, 1939, 213–246). The investigation revealed that the Bell System utilized virtually all of the above patent practices to extend the life and scope of its monopoly. Floyd L. Vaughan (1956) concluded that the patent practices of the Bell System in this period allowed it to completely dominate potential and emerging communication technologies. He states that the Bell System "pre-empts for itself new frontiers of technology for exploitation in the future and, in the meantime, protects what it has already developed. It keeps itself in a commanding position for the exchange of patent rights. In short, it employs patents to maintain its dominance and leadership in communication" (p. 75).

The period of the twenties will not be rehashed to demonstrate the effective relationship between these patent practices and the invention and innovation of communication technologies. Rather, the earlier history of the Bell Telephone Company will be explored. This brief exploration of the early development highlights how the foundation of the Bell System as a corporate enterprise and the design of telephone technology are shaped by the conjuncture between capitalist economic motives and patent law as the legal means whereby property rights in invention are asserted. This example is thus not limited to a demonstration of the operation of the second stage of development, but it rather involves the first stage of development as well. Indeed, in the case of Bell, the two stages are highly compressed. A patent on a single invention is the basis for a monopoly that is, from its inception, caught up in battles to establish dominance over entire sectors of communication.

Patent Practices and the Extension of Monopoly Control: The Bell Telephone Company

Although history heralds Alexander Graham Bell as an inventor of genius, capitalist economic motivation in conjuncture with patent law as the means to obtain property rights in invention had considerable influence on the shape of the telephone and of the system of telephony.[7] The financial support for the development of Bell's telephone work came largely from Gardiner Hubbard, a Boston and Washington attorney with a long background in public utility affairs. Richard Jay Solomon (1978) claims that a careful tracing of Hubbard's antimonopoly lobbying against Western Union and his association with Bell leads to a picture suggesting that Hubbard was interested in undermining the monopoly of Western Union by supporting the development of a superior telegraph technology. It appears, Solomon claims, that:

Bell's marvelous invention came to be but a tool in the hands of financiers to control the communications infrastructure. Hubbard, for example, had backed Bell hoping he would come up with something which could be used to demonstrate WU's intransigence towards any new technology which would tend to make their plant obsolete. Critics had claimed that the telegraph company, as a monopoly, was not interested in improving the "state of the art" (a familiar enough claim by anti-monopolists of any industry) (pp. 147–148).

After United States Telegraph and later American Telegraph merged with Western Union in 1866, the power of Western Union was awesome. These mergers spawned a corporation with incredible monopoly control with a combined capitalization of over $40,000,000 and control of over 37,380 miles of line, 75,686 miles of wire, and 2,250 telegraph offices (Thompson, 1947, 426). Solomon insinuates that the desire for dominance over this powerful monopoly provided the basis of support for Bell's work. Bell was, in fact, charged to work on the harmonic telegraph, that is, a telegraph that could transmit more than one signal at a time. When Bell discovered—presumably by accident—a technique whereby vocal sounds could be transmitted over the telegraph wires, his financiers pushed him and Watson to develop a telephone as a broadcast-like medium. Bell's financiers, anxious for profits, viewed the innovation of a system that delivered music, news, and drama as a potentially profitable enterprise. During 1876 and 1877, Bell and his assistant, Thomas A. Watson, demonstrated telephones designed to operate in such a capacity (Aronson, 1977, 19–21).

Bell became convinced that the telephone would be useful as a form of long-distance communication, but his financiers were initially opposed. Consequently, Bell integrated the role of entrepreneur into his inventive activities. The process of invention and innovation that followed was shaped by the need to render telephony attractive as a capitalist enterprise—specifically to insure that the invention would suit the needs of capitalist economic enterprise. Thus, Bell marketed the telephone system initially as a boon to members of the business community, first to use themselves and then as a profitable business venture to operate.[8] In a letter written "To the Capitalists of the Electric Telephone Company" of England in 1878, Bell made it clear that the larger the number of telephones and the more that they are used in everyday life, the more potential for profit (see Kingsbury, 1915, 89–92). As pointed out by Colin Cherry (1977, pp. 113–114), because the telphone performs an essentially organizational function where there was previously no organization, "it creates *productive* traffic." In his letter to the capitalists, Bell was obviously aware of ways in which the telephone would create such traffic. He stated, for example:

It is probable that such a use of the telephone would speedily become popular, and that as the public became accustomed to the telephone in their houses, they would recognise the advantage of a system of intercommunication. When this time arrives, I would advise the company to place telephones free of charge for a specified period in a few of the principal shops so as to offer to those householders who work with the central office, the additional advantages of oral communication with their tradespeople. The central office system once inaugurated in this manner would inevitably grow to enormous proportions, for those shopkeepers would thus be induced to employ the telephone, and as such connections with the central office increased in number, so would the advantages to householders become more apparent and the number of subscribers increased (quoted in Kingsbury, 1915, p. 91).

It is evident from Bell's appeal that he understood that the more widely the telephone was used, the more potential there was for profit. We can conclude from this that the design of the system to include a phone in every home was at least related to the goal of profitability.

The Bell Telephone Company was organized in 1877. With the formation of this company and the institution of commercial telephone service in the same year, the company employed many techniques that allowed it to extend the life of the patent monopoly and to extend control of the industry beyond the scope of the initial patent monopoly. Bell's initial patent, titled "Improvements in Telegraphy," was issued on March 3, 1876. This basic patent provided a firm foundation for the control of the entire industry. The foundation became virtually impregnable with the issue of Bell's second basic patent in January 1877. This patent covered the crucial combined receiver–transmitter apparatus. The strength of these basic patents effectively blocked legal entrance of competition into the field of telephony.

The licensing agreements into which the Bell System entered bore the stamp of the conscious policy of the Bell System to extend patent control in time and scope. In March 1881, the American Bell Telephone Company issued its first report to shareholders. In this report, the conscious strategy of dominating the industry through licensing agreements was explicated:

> The policy of making only five-year contracts was adopted, in order that our company could have time to learn the best permanent basis for the relations between the company and its licensees, and to see which of them would prove satisfactory as associates. Many applications are now being made for permanent licenses, and we have begun to give such permanent contracts in places where the business is being prosecuted with energy and success in exchange for a substantial interest in the stock of the local companies. By pursuing this plan, the company will gradually acquire a large permanent interest in the telephone business throughout the country, so that you will not be dependent upon royalties for a revenue when the patents shall have expired (quoted in Kingsbury, 1915, p. 184).

Licensees were permitted only to develop district systems. They were prohibited from transmitting between cities or towns. In a contract dated August 9, 1879, this policy was detailed:

> This Company [i.e., the Bell Company] reserves the exclusive right of renting telephones for the purpose of communication between different towns or

cities or of transmitting messages for hire, and of renting telephones to corporations or individuals whose business may be but partially carried on within the territory assigned to you, although one or more of said telephones may be used within the said territory (quoted in Kingsbury, 1915, p. 183).

This control of the long-distance lines has played an extremely important role in maintaining the domination of the telephone monopoly over communication in the United States. To this day, virtually all long-distance communication by wires within the United States takes place over AT&T's long lines.

The Bell Telephone Company was from the beginning involved in the manufacture of telephone equipment. Licensees were not allowed to buy equipment, only rent it. In this way revenues could be collected on a continual basis even after the expiration of the patent. The company was also continually inventing accessories—the bell, for example—which they could then patent and sell or rent to licensees. It became the policy of the company to license other companies to manufacture these accessories and then require exchange licensees—through tie-in clauses in licenses—to purchase the accessories from the licensed manufacturers (Kingsbury, 1915, 184).

Very early in its growth, the Bell System cultivated the strategy of acquiring great numbers of patents that would strategically protect and extend its monopoly control. As early as 1881 the first report to stockholders boasted:

The report of the General Inspector upon this department shows that we own or control, either by purchase or by inventions made by our own electricians, 124 patents, and have applications to the Patent Office for 77 more. Among these a considerable number are of great value as a protection of our business, and from them a substantial revenue has already been received by royalties from our licensees. This source of income will be materially increased, and should eventually more than cover our experimental and electrical expenses (quoted in Kingsbury, 1915, p. 185).

By utilizing such strategies, the Bell Telephone Company extended its control and dominance far beyond the original monopoly bestowed by the 1876 patent. This domination extended beyond the date of the expiration of the original patent. With the expiration of the patent in 1893, rival firms entered the market, and considerable growth occurred in telephony in general (Pierce, 1977, 161). For the most part, however, competitors were relegated to less profitable markets, as the saturation of the profitable markets by the Bell Telephone Company was substantial. Furthermore, the dominance of the Bell interests was so complete that the competition with the new firms actually benefited the Bell system in the long run. Noobar R. Danielian (1939, 14) points out that, as a result of the new competition, telephone rates were forced down, thus expanding demand. Consequently, the Bell System's assets soared.

The shape of the technology the Bell System continually invented—technology that came to define the telephone—conformed to the demands of competition. For example, the development of a superior transmitter by Thomas Edison, while in the employ of Western Union, prompted the rapid development and relevant patent protection for the Bell System's improved transmitter (Kingsbury, 1915, 107–124). Yet a sterling example of the shaping process is afforded by examining the origins of the exchange system, which mirrors the model of centralized control that characterizes AT&T's control even today. Bell argues in the letter to the capitalists that centralized control of the telephone technology offers the best advantage for control and profitability:

> The plan usually presented in regard to private telegraphs is to lease such lines to private individuals, or to companies at a fixed annual rental. This plan should be adopted by you, but instead of erecting a line directly from one to another, I would advise you to bring the wires from the two points to the office of the Company and there connect them together; if this plan be followed a large number of wires would soon be centred in the telephone offices, where they would be easily accessible for testing purposes. . . .
>
> Should this plan be adopted, the company should employ a man in each central office for the purpose of connecting wires as desired. A fixed annual rental could be charged for the use of wires, or a toll could be levied. As all connections would necessarily be made at the central office, it would be easy to note the time during which any wires were connected and to make a charge accordingly—bills could be sent in periodically. However small the rate of charges might be, the revenue would probably be something enormous (quoted in Kingsbury, 1915, pp. 90– 91).

While the idea of an exchange system was neither new nor unique to the Bell System, the Bell Telephone Company was quick to recognize its value in service of the institution's needs, and it was responsible for developing the system and the subsequent inventions that streamlined it. (Kingsbury, 1915, 70–98)

Significant efforts were undertaken to wrest control of the basic Bell patent from Bell. Notably, serious patent challenges were initiated by Elisha Gray and Daniel Drawbraugh. Yet the ideology of invention as embodied in patent law allows for only one inventor; because Bell, with the help of his supporters, was able to establish himself legally as the inventor of the telephone, the basis for the monopoly was firmly established, and others were excluded from having any autonomous ability to determine the shape of telephony.

Thus, both the invention and the inventor become subjugated to capitalist relations of production and in particular to the patent practices utilized in competition between capitalists. Since patent law determines that an invention is the intellectual property of a single individual, Bell's patents could form the basis for monopoly and eventually for the establishment of dominance in the field. In competition with other monopolies, the strongest monopoly, in this case the Bell system, is able to draw upon invention in the monopoly sphere or exclude it from having any autonomous role in determining the shape of communication technologies and systems. The development of the transmitter in response to that developed by Edison provides an example of this process. Furthermore, as the example of the early development of telephony illustrates, technology, as property in the hands of capitalist interests, becomes the means whereby surplus value is acquired and is designed in accordance with that goal. The technology is then further developed and designed in accordance with the need for capital to grow, to expand, and to establish dominance in broad sectors of the market, in this case in communications.

Just as technology is subjugated in capitalist relations of production, the laborer is likewise subjugated in class-dominated relations. Both inventors and the act of invention are subjugated to the needs of capital. Even Bell had to serve the interests of monopoly capital in developing the telephone. Although he became a capitalist himself, in that he owned stock in the early telephone companies, he and his original financiers lost control of the stock and therefore control of the patents on which the companies were built. Having relinquished his property rights in his invention, Bell relinquished any claim to inherent rights in it. There is thus a contradiction—and ultimately competition—between the interests of monopoly capital and the patent rights of an individual inventor.

A number of patent strategies have been developed to acquire the patent rights of individual inventors. One strategy is to bring the inventor into the corporation as labor, a practice that apparently was widespread by the 1920s. This practice serves to rationalize the corporate exploitation of patents. As Machlup (U.S. Congress, 1958b, p. 78) discovered, "the largest research laboratories are in fact maintained by corporations with the strongest patent positions and with high and stable earnings." This strategy also serves to subjugate the inventor as a laborer in capitalist relations of property and appropriation, as discussed earlier. Inventors in these research laboratories are generally hired to perform highly specific duties that conform to the interests of the corporation. In 1940 Alfred E. Kahn (1940, pp. 481–482) described the situation of inventors in large corporations:

inventors are for the most part trained salaried professionals, hired to learn and to work in the great laboratories provided by those who can afford them. Patents are automatically assigned to the corporation which pays the salaries and provides the facilities. . . . When private enterprise provides the means and compensation for research, those who pursue it will fix their attention on what business looks upon as practical tasks and practical results.

While inventors working within corporations are not necessarily likely to obtain more patents,[9] they are likely to have better laboratory facilities, and they will certainly have better patenting facilities and advice. Working in industry can be, as a result, very attractive for an independent inventor. Yet by working for monopoly capital, the inventor's labor power and his or her inventions become the property of monopoly capital.

Not only is labor subjugated as inventor. The operation of corporate enterprise in communication requires laborers of all kinds. For example, in 1885 Bell Telephone companies employed 5,766 workers; in 1930 they employed 324,343 workers, two–thirds of whom were women (Danielian, 1939, 17). As of December 1, 1979 the number of employees of AT&T and its subsidiaries had risen to a phenomenal 1,030,000 (*Moodies*, 1980, 35). These laborers, in selling their labor power to the company, are subjugated in a capitalist class relationship made possible by the monopoly control over telephone technology as intellectual property.

During this stage, as invention moves into the big research laboratories, the role of independent inventor is seriously altered. There is less independent invention, and it is less likely to result in the establishment of an entirely new industry. Because there still is independent invention and independent inventors can still sell or lease inventions and thereby benefit both themselves and industry in general, the patent system is depicted as still promoting progress. Such is the gist of the conclusions made by the Temporary National Economic Committee (TNEC) in 1941 (Folk, 1942, 165– 166). Yet as the testimony before the TNEC suggests, the real benefit in preserving patent rights in the nonmonopoly sector of society is that it actually enhances the position of monopoly capital. Representatives of monopoly capital testifying before the TNEC made it clear that they depended considerably on invention originating outside their own research laboratories. William D. Coolidge, Director of the Research Laboratory of GE, indicated that GE was "always on the lookout for new inventions . . . whether they come from our laboratory or whether they may be from the outside" (Folk, 1942, p. 152). Frank B. Jewett, President of the Bell Telephone Laboratories, expanding on the importance of those inventions that come from outside the research laboratory, claimed that utilizing patents generated outside the organization was absolutely necessary and advantageous. Although Jewett felt that there were certain sectors of invention where the independent inventor had no chance of being effective, he maintained that

there are certain sectors . . . where I think the chances—in our case it happened to be two out of three—in the majority of cases are ten to one, that the very fundamental things are going to come from outside big laboratories, simply because of the nature of things. They are a creation and brain child of particular individuals who have the capacity and knowledge, and heaven knows we could not collar them all, even if we wanted to (quoted in Folk, 1942, p. 158).

Certainly, the desire is not to "collar them all, " but only to collar those inventions that are useful to monopoly capital. As Nicos Poulantzas (1978a) has pointed out, preserving a restricted nonmonopoly capital sector is economically useful to monopoly capital. Two of the reasons for this apply directly to the kind of relationship alluded to by Coolidge and Jewett between independent inventors and the monopolistic research laboratories. The first reason is that, "Monopoly capital often leaves non–monopoly capital the possibility of pioneering new sectors of production, intervening itself only when the risks are minimized; this was the case, to a certain extent, with the electronics and computer industries in the United States and Japan" (p. 142). By thus allowing the nonmonopoly sector to take risks, the monopoly sector is saved from having complete responsibility for technological development, much of which might not prove to be economically useful anyway. A second reason Poulantzas points to is that, "Non-monopoly capital enables monopoly capital to recoup technological innovations at lowest cost. Monopoly capital does not have to finance these in their entirety; several innovations in fact derive from non-monopoly capital, but since this cannot itself apply them, it hands them over to monopoly capital in the form of patents" (pp. 142– 143).

Thus the patent system, in promising equal legal status and protection to independent and/or nonmonopoly inventors, provides encouragement to risk time, energy, and money in the development of inventions. Yet due to the superior economic position of monopoly capital, it is much easier for the large corporation to assure extensive development and innovation of the invention and thereby exploit the patent. So, the big communication corporations are virtually free to wait and choose what they do or do not want to develop, leaving the risks involved in invention to others. The outside inventors are in a decidedly vulnerable position. Development and innovation often require many more resources than inventors can marshal. Thus, if they desire to see their invention developed and innovated, they may need to seek out support from monopoly capital through the sale or lease of their patent rights. Of course, corporate motivations might differ considerably from those of the inventors, and the industry will more likely evaluate the invention in terms of its potential marketability, its potential threat to the corporate market, and its potential as a bargaining chip. If rights to the invention are acquired, the intent may be to suppress the invention or to alter it significantly as much as it might be to adopt it. The overall consequence of this dynamic is that nonmonopoly invention ceases for the most part to play the role of an autonomous social force.

Patent Practices and the Nonmonopoly Inventor: Joseph Tykociner

The mechanism whereby industry can "collar" outside invention is illustrated by the attempts of Joseph Tykociner to develop and innovate his sound-on-film invention in the 1920s.[10] Tykociner had worked on the development of sound-on-film techniques as an individual inventor without significant institutional and/or financial backing since 1896. Until he came to the University of Illinois in 1921, he had been unable to test the inventions he had carried in his imagination and explored on paper. Because he believed himself to be in the forefront of invention (due to this working in relative isolation), and perhaps because of naiveté, Tykociner did not take the necessary steps to establish a strong patent position as early as he should have. He neither submitted any patent applications nor actually constructed a working model of any one of his ideas until coming to the university. Nor did he take special care to develop and protect his patent applications with an adequate range of claims when he did finally submit them. As a result, his patent applications were submitted late and offered questionable coverage when examined vis-à-vis competing patents. Nonetheless, by early 1922 Tykociner had built and demonstrated a workable optical sound-on-film system.

It was customary at that time for a faculty member to assign to the university patent rights to inventions created while at the university. Tykociner was not required to do so since he was able to prove to the university's satisfaction that his formulation of the various processes of sound recording and reproduction had taken place long before he came to the university. The university would not support continued research, however, unless Tykociner was willing to turn over the patent rights. Tykociner wanted very much to see his invention developed and innovated, and he was willing to turn over any possible patents provided that the university would guarantee such development. Tykociner was astute enough to recognize that the initial invention was not enough to form the basis for commercial development. More work needed to be done, technicalities had to be worked out, and patents had to be developed and defended. Unfortunately, he was unable to strike a satisfactory agreement with the university, and Tykociner was ordered to halt research on university time using university facilities.

Although Tykociner wanted to see his invention developed commercially, he preferred that it be developed by interests other than the big monopoly corporations. Throughout the spring, summer, and fall of 1922 he corresponded with a myriad of law firms wanting to incorporate him, with public relations firms wanting to help him rationalize publicity, with individuals wishing to invest and assist in commercial development of his invention, and with inventors of related inventions desiring to make either trades or deals whereby they and sometimes Tykociner might benefit. None of these contacts materialized into any agreements that might insure commercial development.

By August of 1922, it became clear to Tykociner that he was not the only inventor working in the field. In a letter dated August 17 to Jacob Chaitkin, he expressed the belief that "the field will belong to the man who will gain the most of the experience by research and practical applications going hand in hand." In a telegram sent to Chaitkin on the same day, he wrote that "A NEW ART IS STARTED THOSE WHO WILL CONTINUE DEVELOPING WILL HAVE THE FRUITS" (Box 20). During the early summer, Tykociner must have sensed that commercial development of the kind he envisioned was hopeless, for he began sending out feelers to the monopolies he had hoped to avoid. In June he contacted a friend at the Eastman Kodak Company, Ludwig Silberstein, hinting that Kodak might be interested. On June 16, Silberstein wrote back that the director of the research laboratory at Kodak "states that the Eastman Kodak Company would not be inclined to take any interest in the commercial exploitation of photographic reproduction of sound in connection with motion pictures or the phonograph" (Box 20).

When the situation seemed desperate by late 1922, Tykociner initiated contacts and began negotiating with Westinghouse, GE, and AT&T's subsidiary, Western Electric. All of these companies expressed interest in his invention—particularly in the strength of his patent position. Representatives from each of the companies had long meetings with Tykociner, witnessed demonstrations of the apparatus, and reviewed Tykociner's patent postion. Westinghouse was interested. In a letter dated January 18, 1923, O. S. Schairer (Westinghouse's Director of Patent Development) offered a payment of $1,140 for any patents received, a job for Tykociner at a salary of $300 per month plus 5-percent royalties for possible licensing operations. By return letters on January 22 and February 28 Tykociner bargained for $1,800, a salary of $420, and 5-percent royalties with a minimum royalty of $4,000 per year. The final stipulation of a minimum royalty was a particularly important one for Tykociner because it signified a degree of assurance that the company would seek to undertake commercial development of his work in a serious way. Additionally, it assured Tykociner that he would not

suffer in case the Company abstains entering extensively into the business, no matter how good my results may be; or in case the Company decides some day to give up entirely this line in order to achieve instead concessions in a other branch of business by an understanding with a competing concern (Box 20).

Westinghouse evidently didn't feel that it needed Tykociner or his patents that badly, maintaining throughout later correspondence that Tykociner's desire for money and minimum royalty guarantees represented a lack of confidence in his inventions. The Director of Patent Development at Westinghouse wrote to Tykociner on February 23,

we believe that the best evidence of your confidence in your inventions would be your willingness to begin work with us for a moderate compensation and your willingness to rely upon the practical results that you can produce with your inventions by developing them at our expense and with our facilities (Box 20).

Correspondence eventually dropped off with Westinghouse, which informed Tykociner of a patent that they apparently assumed would undermine Tykociner's ability to obtain solid protection.

Shortly after contacting Westinghouse, Tykociner approached the General Electric Company. GE was interested, probably because Charles A. Hoxie, who was working for GE, claimed to have invented a workable sound-on-film system. The representatives from GE, like those at Westinghouse, expressed concern over the patent situation and requested that Tykociner bring all his patent applications when he visited the company in Schenectady. GE engineer, L. A. Hawkins, in December of 1922, maintained that the "patent situation seems to be quite complicated" (Box 20). After a demonstration and after examining Tykociner's patent applications, GE terminated correspondence.

Finally, in March 1923, Jack C. R. Palmer from Western Electric's Patents Department came to Urbana to discuss the technical details and patent situation of Tykociner's work. By early April, Western Electric had decided that it was not interested either. In a letter dated April 12, Palmer summed up the company's position in these terms:

it appears that any payment which we might make for rights to your inventions would, in view of the present state of the art, be wholly in the nature of speculation. On this basis we could not justify a payment at all commensurate with the value which you undoubtedly attach to your inventions (Box 20).

After a few more attempts at making arrangements with smaller concerns throughout the summer, Tykociner finally gave up.

The reason the monopolies were interested in Tykociner's invention is not clear, but it is clear that it had something to do with obtaining a secure patent position—and, in the case of Western Electric, perhaps a perfected invention as well. Tykociner could offer neither of these, for as he was well aware, more work was required to perfect, protect, and market his invention on a large scale. The support for such work was withheld. Furthermore, it is clear that representatives of the monopoly interests were able to examine and discuss in detail not only the apparatus Tykociner had constructed and the various patent applications associated with it (applications are not required to be made public), but also the technical specifications of a number of other inventions that Tykociner hoped to reduce to practice. Thus, the monopoly interests would have been able to determine whether Tykociner's patent situation was strong enough to use competitively, with or without ever intending to develop the invention. They were also given the opportunity to appropriate any number of Tykociner's ideas. Tykociner certainly did not have the ability to monitor what the companies did with his ideas. Having thus gotten all that they could, and deciding that it wasn't worth giving him any support, they dismissed Tykociner.

Tykociner's case is particularly interesting in that it demonstrates the vulnerability of the nonmonopoly inventor who, without sufficient resources and institutional support, can provide monopoly capital with new raw material either to establish or to extend monopoly control in communications. In Tykociner's case, this occurred at great expense to him—financially and emotionally. He finally received only a few minor patents and is rarely recognized as an important inventor in the development of sound-on-film. Yet as is sometimes the case when an inventor does establish a strong patent position, monopoly capital is still able to appropriate the inventor's work, having let the nonmonopoly inventor incur great cost and risk. Either by purchasing patent rights or by stealing the invention, monopoly capital can benefit greatly from developments in the nonmonopoly sector. Examples of these kinds dot the pages of the history of communication technologies. So, for example, most of the important inventions with which Bell Telephone protected its monopoly throughout the early 1900s came from inventors in the nonmonopoly sectors whose patent rights were purchased by AT&T

———

(Danielian, 1939, 98–100). Similarly, it is not uncommon to find evidence to the effect that monopoly interests are able to steal inventions with relative ease. A sterling example is RCA's blatant theft of Edwin Armstrong's inventions in the development of FM. The Armstrong case is illustrative precisely because his patents were very strong and he had considerable resources with which to fight RCA's infringement of them.

Patent Practices and the Theft of Inventions: Edwin Armstrong

Between July 1930 and January 1933, Edwin Armstrong, with the aid of patent lawyers, carefully drew up and submitted patent applications on a frequency modulation (FM) radio signaling system that virtually eliminated static and was capable of revolutionizing radio transmission.[11] In December 1933, Armstrong was issued four patents on these applications, and he was later to receive many more. These patents were tight enough to give Armstrong's invention a strong legal position from which to challenge infringement. Armstrong, as one of the largest stockholders at the time in RCA, offered to license his patents to RCA. RCA stalled and even attempted to suppress the development of FM so that it might not present any serious competition for frequencies that RCA wanted for television. Yet the technical superiority of FM, along with the vigor and financial strength of Armstrong, made it difficult for RCA to suppress the invention. Throughout the late 1930s interest grew in FM. Numerous small interests were licensed to use the FM patents, as were GE and Western Electric. In January 1940, Armstrong and an independent FM Broadcasters Association convinced the FCC to hold up frequency allocations for television until FM's needs were considered. At this, RCA decided to strike an agreement with Armstrong. David Sarnoff, President of RCA, proposed that for $1 million, RCA be given a nonexclusive license on the FM patents without having to pay royalties. Armstrong rejected this offer on the basis that it was unfair to other interests that were paying royalties. RCA refused to pay royalties and would not therefore pay for license rights to Armstrong's patents.

Instead, RCA, it has been suggested, simply stole Armstrong's invention. RCA had been working on and patenting a new system of FM since 1936, which they hoped would compete with Armstrong's. Stuart W. Seeley, while working for RCA, developed a receiver circuit called the "ratio detector" in 1942, and in 1946 RCA marketed a line of FM radios that utilized this development. Armstrong and others demonstrated that the ratio detector infringed Armstrong's patents by doing nothing more than combining "the functions of limiting and discrimination in a single tube operation, embodying no new principles. . . . Not only did it embody no new principles, but it embodied old principles in such a way as to give something less than full FM performance and noise reduction" (Lessing, 1956, p. 276). RCA claimed that the invention was different from Armstrong's, persuading licensees that there was no infringement of his patents. On July 22, 1948, Armstrong filed suit against RCA and NBC for infringing his patents as well as for inducing others to infringe them. An eight-year battle ensued, during which time the power and resources of RCA were pitched against those of Armstrong. The battle depleted Armstrong's financial, physical, and mental resources, and on January 31, 1954, he committed suicide. In December 1954, the case was settled, and the Armstrong estate was awarded a mere $1 million, with many of the royalties owed to Armstrong remaining uncollected.

As the examples of Tykociner and Armstrong illustrate, it is useful and possible for monopoly interests to dominate invention in the nonmonopoly sector. To this end, the patent system is a useful tool. Of course, once a patent right is obtained, an invention stolen, or the competitive situation merely assessed, technologies are developed, further developed, or suppressed in accordance with the economic interests of monopoly capital.

In sum, the second stage of development of the relationship between patent law and the invention and innovation of communication technologies is characterized by the coordinated development and utilization of technologies and patents to meet the new demands of monopoly capital in the quest to establish, expand, and maintain dominance over entire sectors of communications. The effectivity of this conjuncture is such that patented communication inventions become the tools of capital in competitive practices between individual capitalists and between entire branches of industry. In the desire to monopolize invention, monopoly capital not only subjugates invention, but also inventors and the practice of invention by creating research laboratories where inventors are mere laborers who are required to assign their inventions to the company. In addition, the role of nonmonopoly invention becomes subjugated to monopoly capital, for it is a source of new material that is readily available at reduced risk and cost to monopoly capital.

As a consequence of these developments in the second stage, technologies and systems are designed to suit not only the needs of capitalist economic production, but also to suit the kind of competition that characterizes late capitalism. In so doing, labor, the means of communicating, communication situations, and invention and innovation in communication are yet further subjugated in capitalist relations of domination.

THE IMPENDING THIRD STAGE OF THE RELATIONSHIP BETWEEN PATENT LAW AND THE INVENTION AND INNOVATION OF COMMUNICATION TECHNOLOGIES AND SYSTEMS

That we may be entering a third stage in the relationship between patents and the invention and innovation of communication technologies is largely speculative. The speculation is based on the growing concern of scholars, lawyers, and industrialists for the legal protection of property in what has been deemed the impending "information age." The information age, as characterized by Edwin B. Parker (1976, p. 5), is one in which "the characteristic machine is one that processes information, augmenting not human physical energy but human information processing." Many of the inventions of this new age will be protected easily by patent law. Computer hardware, for example, fits quite nicely the requirements for invention as required by patent law. Predictably, computer companies are currently jostling to establish dominance in the field on national and international levels, with International Business Machines (IBM) well in the lead (Schiller, 1978). Other forms of information, however, that are of potentially invaluable economic interest to monopoly capital, do not clearly come under the purview of invention to be protected by patent law. For example, computer software—in particular, programs—is a form of information that industry hopes can be protected by patent law. Although the outlook is not particularly promising, there is currently an attempt, either to make software fit existing definitions of invention or to change the law so that it covers software.

Patents and the Protection of Computer Software

The impetus for seeking protection for computer software is predictably the desire to benefit economically from the production and marketing of software. As the computer industry has matured, the pre-eminent commodity it develops and markets has been steadily shifting from computer hardware to software. In the early development of the computing industry, software was relatively uncomplicated and inexpensive to develop. Computer firms routinely provided incentive to purchase hardware by including free software. Users who developed their own software often shared their programs freely as well. As programming became more complex in the 1960s, the development of software became more difficult, time-consuming, and expensive. While improvements continued to be made in the hardware, the real innovations were more and more in the creation of increasingly sophisticated software (Sutter, 1976). Users came to rely more on the software developed by others, and eventually companies began marketing their software separately. Firms specializing in the production and distribution of software entered the market in the 1970s, and currently mass-marketed software packages are readily available from both hardware producers and independent software producers.

Software has become an extremely important source of revenue for the computer industry. Archie McGill, Vice President of Business Marketing at AT&T, has predicted that software "will become the backbone of the communications process by the mid '80s" (quoted in, Myers, 1979a, p. 51). Although estimates vary considerably, annual revenues from software products have been estimated as high as $52 billion, and the growth per year for the next five years at 27 percent (Goetz, 1979, 136). In 1978 the World Peace through Law Center (1978, 3) estimated that 70 percent of all computer expenditures were for software as opposed to 30 percent for hardware, and an earlier estimate indicated that the cost was quickly approaching a figure of 90 percent for software and personnel as opposed to 10 percent for hardware (U.S. Department of Commerce, 1977, 47). Yet, while software has become a primary source of revenue, it has also required more investment of time and money. Software production is highly labor-intensive, and as there has been a shortage of highly qualified programmers who demand increasingly higher wages, there has been a corresponding increase in the cost of programming (Goetz, 1979). In addition, most large-scale software takes one to three years to develop, and its usefulness is usually limited to six to ten years (Putnam & Fitzsimmons, 1979, 137). This combination of factors—the increasing prominence of software as a revenue producer, along with the increasing costs of development and maintenance—has led industry to seek ways to insure return on investment in the development of software, as well as to adopt ways to develop and control the software product so as to insure maximum profitability. It has become a paramount concern of industry to protect the investment in software by asserting property rights in it.

Patent protection is a particularly attractive form of protection for software because a patentee can maintain control over a program through license agreements, and, in addition, it can prohibit the use of such a program by a third party even if it is developed independently. Early attempts to patent programs *qua* programs were rejected by the Patent Office based on the belief that the subject matter was nonstatutory; that is, a computer program did not meet the criteria for "invention." Attempts to obtain patent protection for programs as something other than programs ensued. In particular, the hope was that, by claiming that programs were processes or machine components, the claimants could be extended protection under existing law (U.S. President's Commission on the Patent System, 1966, 13).

The advisability of extending patent protection to include computer software—regardless of how it was defined—was questioned within the government and within the Patent Office. The issue was, as a result, a primary concern of the President's Commission on the Patent System, which was established on April 8, 1965. The Commission's recommendations (U.S. President's Commission on the Patent System, 1966), submitted to President Johnson on November 17, 1966, included a strong statement to the effect that computer programs should not be protected by patent law regardless of how they were defined:

A series of instructions which control or condition the operation of a data processing machine, generally referred to as a "program," shall not be considered patentable regardless of whether the program is claimed as (a) an article, (b) a process described in terms of the operations performed by a machine pursuant to a program, or (c) one or more machine configurations established by a program (p. 12).

Two reasons were given for this decision: (1) that the present statute simply did not provide adequate and certain grounds for protection, and (2) that the Patent Office wasn't equipped to search the prior art and classify computer programs (U.S. President's Commission on the Patent System, 1966, 13). Computer software represented an entirely new kind of information, which did not clearly fit the existing definitions of machines or processes that the Patent Office held to be patentable. In addition, the Patent Office was simply ill-equipped to deal with the demands that granting protection would generate. The Commission's recommendations were highly controversial, and in 1968 legislation proposed to implement its recommendations was withdrawn (Nycum, 1978, 63).

Although it is not certain when the first software patent was issued, it is generally accepted that it was issued to Martin Goetz in June 1968 (Goetz, 1978, 25; Nycum, 1978, 75–76). The issue of this patent and the subsequent discussion of the implications of its issue seem to have caused some consternation within the Patent Office. There was renewed concern within the Office about the possible consequences of extending protection to computer software, after which the Patent Office became decidedly opposed to patenting software (Nycum, 1978, 75).

The issue of patentability has remained unsettled; the primary locus of the debate has been within case law, not within statutory law. The more significant cases, along with the legal issues that they raise, have been exhaustively covered elsewhere (Kurtz, 1978; Lowe, 1979a and 1979b; Nycum, 1978; Pfeifer, 1978; Popper, 1977). In summary, the situation, as it appears in the literature, is that the Patent Office is reticent to issue any patents on computer software or software-related inventions—such as machine configurations established by a program. This reticence is based primarily on the grounds that it is not legitimate to extend protection to innovations in mathematical procedures—something that has been held to since the middle of the nineteenth century (Lowe, 1979a, 2).

The Court of Customs and Patent Appeals (CCPA), however, to which appeals can be made and which has supervisory authority over the Patent Office, has demonstrated a much more liberal attitude toward the patenting of software and software-related inventions. The situation is still further complicated by the fact that, in the three cases considered by the Supreme Court that involved computer programs, the Court declared the programs unpatentable.[12] Unfortunately, these cases are not definitive, for the Court did not address directly the question of patentability of programs in general. In two of these cases (*Gottschalk* and *Parker*), the Court stated explicitly that its decision did not preclude altogether the possibility of patenting programs. As it currently stands, however, the Supreme Court would not uphold a patent on a program that could be deemed a patent on a mathematical algorithm (*Gottschalk*) or on an obvious process based on new or old mathematics (*Parker*). Protection for programs is limited, at best, to the extent that they can be protected as computer components or as industrial processes, and not as algorithms. If a program is built into the hardware, a patent might be obtained. Some commentators have even suggested that all programs should be defined as computer components and thus deserve protection (Goetz, 1978). In March 1981, the Supreme Court ruled in *Diamond v. Diehr,* in a five-to-four vote, that an industrial process designed around a computer program was patentable as long as the entire process was new. While this case enlarges the possibilities for protecting computer software somewhat, it still does not settle the issue.[13]

There is some hesitancy within both the computer software industry and the legal profession to press too hard for resolution to the problem of defining computer software. Once a definition has been adopted by the courts, it may well exclude computer programs from certain forms of protection—one of which is patent protection (Keet, 1979; Myers, 1979b). There is still considerable hope that case law might be able to establish patent protection. It does not bode well, however, that there is an international trend toward the refusal to recognize computer programs as patentable. In many countries where the situation has been resolved, notably in the Federal Republic of Germany and in France,

———

programs have been held to be unpatentable. In addition, in 1973 the European Economic Community expressly excluded computer programs from protection by the European Economic Patent Grant System (Pagenberg, 1974).

Comprehensive patent protection without new federal legislation is still questionable. Given the discrepancy between the policies of the Patent Office, the CCPA, and the Supreme Court, protection is not guaranteed. The answer for many of those interested in assuring patent protection therefore lies in federal legislation. It is fairly common for both those in and out of government to call for a resolution of the issue through legislation (see, for example, Lowe, 1979a, 14). Even the Supreme Court has called for congressional resolution of the issue (see Nycum, 1978, 64).

Predictably, the justification for calling for protection of computer software is based on the desire to protect capital investment. One lawyer (Lowe, 1979a, p. 14) has called upon professionals to urge Congressmen and Senators to settle the matter, "If you feel that the investment and effort your company has put into computer programs should be protected by patents, as well as by other legal mechanisms, such as trade secrets and copyrights." Yet the basis for the claim that these particular investments deserve protection as property rights is still very much related to the idea that an individual's ideas are inherently property. Dan McCracken, computer scientist and author, has claimed that, "A computer program is as much an intellectual property as anything else and a guy who's slaved over a program for a year or more has a right to protect it" (quoted in Myers, 1978, p. 125). Overlooked is the fact that, to begin with, the law took the relatively unformed notion of inherent rights and elevated it to its currently effective status as intellectual property.

In the light of the failure of patent law to provide explicit protection, it may fall out of the picture altogether as a means to assert property rights in this increasingly important economic entity. In fact, industry, lawyers, and scholars are exploring the possibility that the protection of property rights in computer software might better be obtained by utilizing other forms of law that have been designed to protect intellectual property, notably copyright and trade secret law. If patent protection is eventually granted, the strategies by which the definitions of computer software and ad hoc legal arrangements are made to correspond will extend protection to ideas beyond those areas that have been traditionally granted such protection. Such an extension is highly desirable to industry, but it would also grant industry the ability to control ideas and the means of communication on a scale previously unachievable (Slack, 1981).

Either patent law may change to accommodate the needs of industry, or its effectivity in relationship to this new, third stage of development may be considerably diminished. Regardless of which path it follows, the likelihood that there will be a change reveals finally that a crucial conjuncture is at those points where ideas are defined in law as intellectual property at the behest of the interests of monopoly capital. Patent law does not protect property rights in the abstract category of "ideas" per se. It does, however, elevate certain ideas that meet historically determined criteria to the status of "invention," and it does protect property rights in those inventions. Such has been the case since the beginning of patent law, when weaving designs were protected by patent rights. It is merely a question of determining which ideas, under which circumstances, "deserve" protection. Currently, the extension of patent rights to heretofore unprotected kinds of ideas would extend the ability of monopoly capital to subjugate labor, the means of communicating, communication situations, and invention and innovation in communication in capitalist relations of domination.

INTERVENTION IN THE RELATIONSHIP BETWEEN PATENT LAW AND THE INVENTION AND INNOVATION OF COMMUNICATION TECHNOLOGIES AND SYSTEMS

As analysis indicates, the tendency has been toward increasing domination of invention, inventors, and the act of invention by monopoly capital. As a consequence, communication technologies and systems are not invented and innovated in response to critical assessment of human communication needs. Nor, for that matter, are they invented and innovated in response to any semblence of a critical analysis of the political, economic, and ideological constituents of their relationship to society. Letting the self-serving interests of capital define for us so thoroughly how we communicate and the means for communicating must be considered highly undesirable. As the analysis has demonstrated, by leaving this precious resource in the hands of capital, we have served only to devalue individual inventors and other laborers, inventions, and the kind and quality of communication technologies and systems in capitalist relations of domination.

Patent law, in codifying a legal and ideological basis for the ownership of ideas in invention, has provided the foundation for that domination. The recommended goal of intervention in the relationship between patent law and the invention and innovation of communication technologies is therefore the abolition of patent law. By eliminating patent law, the crucially effective conjuncture between the juridical, the ideological, and the economic would be altered. This change would make it more difficult for capital to dominate and control—legally and ideologically—

inventions, inventors, and the act of invention. It would still be possible to own technologies, but not to own property rights to the invention itself. Similarly, firms could still hire inventors, but they could not monopolize rights to their employees' inventions. Furthermore, if firms could not own and thereby monopolize inventions, the shape of communication technologies and systems would not be determined so thoroughly by the interests of capital. There could be more room for the success of those inventors and innovators who do consider primarily human communication needs and who design communication technologies and systems in order to emancipate human beings rather than exploit them.

Unfortunately, by eliminating the patent system, we might jeopardize the ability of small, noncapitalist interests to profit from their inventions. Yet we must first recognize that small, noncapitalist interests rarely profit significantly from their inventions anyway. Second, we must resist the temptation to consider any technological development as inherently good. We must be willing to question the kind of development that occurs only when it can be protected as property.

To have a significant impact, the abolition of patent law would have to be accompanied by the abolition of alternative means of obtaining property rights in invention. The problem is not patent law per se, but the ideological, political, and economic constituents of intellectual property. Thus, we would have to be certain that patent law wasn't simply substituted with some other mechanism that would accomplish essentially the same end.

While arguing for the elimination of property rights in invention may be a step toward the abolition of capitalist relations of domination in communications, it probably isn't realistic to expect that patent law will be abolished in response to the input of "right reason." A specific location for intervention is needed, one where we could begin to "chip away" at the ideological constitution of property rights in invention. Just such a location presents itself in the current attempts to extend property rights to computer software.

As stated earlier, the arguments for extending patent protection to computer software are typically based on an appeal to inherent rights. It is argued that individuals have a right to protect their investments in the development of inventions by claiming property rights to ideas that are inherently their own. This argument can be refuted on two grounds. First, from within the position's own ideological orientation, we can demonstrate that patent law does not and cannot protect inherent rights very well. Many examples, such as those of Tykociner and Armstrong, illustrate that noncapitalist and sometimes even capitalist interests are not really guaranteed protection. In the cases where a number of people independently invent similar inventions at about the same time, only one person can be awarded the patent right. Daniel Drawbraugh, for example, was an inventor of telephone technology who was effectively excluded from exercising his inherent or property rights in his invention because he was denied a patent on it. By thus demonstrating that there is an inconsistency or contradiction between property rights and inherent rights, it is clear that patents do not really protect inherent rights anyway.

The argument that patent rights should be extended to computer software on the grounds that individuals have the right to protect their inherent rights can also be refuted by pointing precisely to the ideological nature of the argument. As already demonstrated, the notion of inherent property rights is constituted by the law to begin with. It is therefore tautological to justify the right to protect inherent rights on legal grounds when it is precisely those legal grounds that ultimately create those rights. In making a decision regarding the extension of patent rights to computer software, we must therefore consider and critique the effectivity of the conjuncture of political, ideological, and economic elements as they relate to the issue of extending patent protection.

The political level, as noted, functions to lend coherence to the uneven development of a social formation. One of the political functions of patent law is, and historically has been, to grant privileges that are determined to be in the best interests of a particular social formation. So it is entirely appropriate to approach the problem of extending property rights by questioning whether the extension of rights to include heretofore unprotected information is acting in the best interests of the United States and the world. Clearly the economic elite will claim that it is, because it is in their interest to have a mechanism whereby they control information for their economic benefit. As Edwin Parker with Porat (1976, p. 106) asserted at the Organization for Economic Cooperation and Development's Conference on Computer and Telecommunications Policy in 1975, a major juridico-political problem of the information age will be "trying to make information more or less fit an economic system designed for physical commodities." Yet industry's claims, motivated by economic interest, are based largely on the ideology of industrialization. As Oppenheim (1951, p. 567), in a defense of the American patent system, has maintained, any changes in the patent system are unacceptable if they sacrifice what he has deemed the "workable competitive system" and "American technological supremacy." This ideological and economic role of the patent system in the support of technological development in the service of capitalist economic growth is strongly held to by defenders of the extension of property rights to computer software. As Ernest E. Keet (1979, p. 11), President and Chief Executive Officer of Turnkey Systems, Inc., has argued, "It is clear that the software product industry could quickly vanish if protection mechanisms were not available to the vendors." He continues by maintaining that fostering this protection is in the best interest of customers because it provides a greater level of innovation at reduced costs. We must, however, set aside the ideology of industrialization and argue against commitment to development of invention for its own sake and against the position that competition will provide the impetus to so invent. As Chapter 2 pointed out, the ideology of industrialization involves reasoning and practices that do not address critically the effectivity of communication technologies and systems. Once the ideology of industrialization is discredited, the point asserting some relationship between patent protection and the amount of invention is moot.

Clearly what we would be doing by extending property rights to computer software is providing new tools for the capitalist control of the means and relations of production in communication. The computer industry has made it clear that it is, in fact, seeking exactly that. Members of that industry want to protect their investment in property, but, to do so, software and the invention of software have to be subsumed in capitalist relations of production. Already the industry has developed appropriate technologies, such as centralized computers designed to appropriate surplus value and to exert centralized control over the network. Similarly, as pointed out in Chapter 3, they have learned to appropriate the developments of the Alternative Technology movement to enhance their market control. Their superior economic position, overdetermined in part by tendencies of patent law to promote the monopolization of technologies and technological growth, makes it easier for them, again using patent law, to protect ownership rights and to gain control over inventions developed by smaller capitalist and noncapitalist interests.

Having discredited any appeal to inherent property rights and the ideology of industrialization, we can argue more effectively against the extension of protection on political grounds. Using the logic of the information society theorists and apologists themselves, let us assume that we are indeed entering a new information age, in which information and not the commodities of manufacturing prevail. In that case, we must question whether we want that information to be controlled by forces whose interests are predominantly economic and whose political and ideological consequences subjugate both workers (including inventors) and invention in exploitative relationships. We must question whether that is what we want because that is exactly what is enhanced by the extension of property rights in computer software. Furthermore, once the precedent is set for the extension of protection, it opens the possibility for the extension of protection to still new forms of information that are as yet unprotected. Assuming, of course, that we do not want to provide capital with additional tools with which to dominate our lives and our means of communicating, we should deny extending patent rights to computer software.

CONCLUSION

This intervention is admittedly a relatively small one. Furthermore, this intervention would make sense only if it were conducted in conjunction with an effort to eliminate the possibility that software could be protected as property by other means, most notably by copyright and trade secret law. Even if the intervention were successful, it is not going to alter entirely the effectivity of the relationship between patent law and the invention and innovation of communication technologies in the capitalist mode of production. However, by challenging the practice of granting property rights in one area—particularly in an area as economically important as computer software—we generate practices that embody an ideology that some ideas are not inherently the property rights of individuals. In so doing, we can perhaps lay the groundwork for demanding that the practice of granting property rights in any invention is politically unacceptable. Hopefully, we could gradually mount a significant challenge to the hegemony of the capitalist definition and control of communication technologies and systems and the subjugation of labor, inventions, inventors, and the act of invention in exploitative relationships.

NOTES

[1] The following discussion of the origins of Venetian patent law relies heavily on Prager (1944; 1952). The interpretation is, however, my own.

[2] The entire text of the Patent Act of 1790 is quoted and discussed in Federico (1932, 250–252).

[3] This clause of the Patent Act of 1952 is quoted and compared with the English positive right in Klitzke (1959, 616).

[4] For a more thorough discussion of this process, whereby law and ideology serve to provide a unity but keep people divided in such a way that the dominant class is kept in power, see Poulantzas (1978b, 123–137, 190–194).

[5] See Vaughan (1956), much of which is devoted to the ways in which patent practices of companies contribute to the increased concentration of corporate control. This book includes an extensive bibliography of government documents, court cases, books, pamphlets, and periodical literature, many of which address the use of patent law in competi-

tive practices. See also U.S. Congress (1958a). This is an extensive annotated bibiliography of 446 entries, many of which address the use of patents in competitive practices.

[6] The following description of tactics relies heavily on Machlup's work (U.S. Congress, 1958b, 10–12).

[7] This history of the telephone is based largely on several sources: Kingsbury (1915); Danielian (1939); Coon (1939); and Brooks (1975).

[8] Aronson (1977, 27) has suggested that this marketing strategy may have been based on the model of the telegraph as primarily a service to business.

[9] Schmookler (1972, 40) has demonstrated that, based on the number of patents issued and the number of important inventions, big firms contribute *less* in proportion to their size than individual inventors.

[10] This account of Tykociner's attempt to develop and innovate his invention is based on documents in the Tykociner Files, University of Illinois Archives, Urbana, Illinois. Most of the pertinent information is in Box 20.

[11] The following account of RCA's theft of Armstrong's inventions in FM is based on Lessing (1956, 193–311).

[12] *Dann, Commissioner of Patents and Trademarks v. Johnston,* 425 US 219 (1976); *Gottschalk, Acting Commissioner of Patents v. Benson et al.,* 409 US 63 (1972); *Parker, Acting Commissioner of Patents and Trademarks v. Flook,* US, 57 L Ed 2nd 451 (1978).

[13] For a discussion of *Diamond v. Diehr,* see Kern (1981).

section four

chapter nine

Communications Revolutions: Causality and Intervention

The preceding pages presented a critique of current notions and perspectives on communication technologies. The critique demonstrated that those notions and perspectives are inadequate as bases for critical and comprehensive understanding of the relationship between communication technologies and society and as bases for effective strategies for technological intervention. The aim was to show that the failings of such notions can be explained in part in terms of the concepts of causality embedded in their analyses and practice. Explicated in contrast to inadequate conceptions of causality was a particular theory of structural causality, which is able to overcome the deficiencies of the previous models and to form the basis for a critical and comprehensive inquiry into the relationship between communication technologies and society and subsequent strategies for intervention. Applying structural causality to a concrete instance—the relationship between patent law and the invention and innovation of communication technologies—demonstrated the explanatory power of a structural causal approach in analyzing the relationship between the social formation and communication technologies. On the basis of this analysis, particular dominant elements of the relationship that were judged to be undesirable were located and critiqued. The analysis and the critique suggest that an effective strategy for intervention must involve the abolition of property rights in invention.

Once we understand the integral relationship between models of causality, conceptions of technology, and strategies for intervention, rethinking some of our most deeply held prejudices about communication technologies are in order. For example, the concept of the communication revolution must now be understood in an entirely new light.

Many discussions about communication technologies and society use as their organizing principle the notion of communication revolutions. Today when researchers write about communication technologies, they commonly cast the discussion in terms of revolutionary change. We, as readers, are bombarded with claims for the computer revolution, the home computer revolution, the information revolution, the home video revolution, the cable television revolution, and on and on. Historians write about the print revolution, the electronic revolution, the electric revolution, the transistor revolution, or even something broadly conceived as the communications revolution. This interesting phenomenon—this attribution of revolution to changes in communication technologies—deserves careful critical analysis. Although this brief space does not permit us to trace the historical determinants of the attribution, it does allow an illustration that the attribution is deeply rooted in mechanistic and expressive approaches to the causal relationship between communication technologies and society. Consequently, the attribution must be rejected and replaced by an orientation that is suited to critical analysis and intervention.

While this notion of the communication revolution is generally used with very little precision or consistency of meaning, it nonetheless involves an implicit position on the causal relationship between communication technologies and society. Raymond Williams (1976, p. 229), in exploring the use of the term "revolution" in *Keywords*, explains that, politically, the term has come to mean the bringing about of a whole new social order. Outside a political context, however, the term has come to "indicate fundamental changes, or fundamentally new developments, in a very wide range of activities." In writings about communication revolutions, the phrase usually expresses the latter sense of revolution, in that the communication technologies in question are assumed to be fundamentally different. Yet what in fact makes them fundamentally different is that they are revolutionary in the first sense; that is, these technologies are somehow linked to the bringing about of a whole new social order.

From a simple causal perspective, the revolutionary process results when a so-deemed fundamentally different technology affects virtually all aspects of society and radically transforms it. Typical are these revolutionary claims for the home computer:

The United States—indeed, the world—is about to be totally changed by a revolution few people have seen coming. The corporate world is unprepared for it. The public is unprepared for it. Governments are unprepared for it. And it will remake our world as drastically as the automobile, the telephone, or the atomic bomb.

It is the home computer revolution (Nelson, 1977, p. 10).

A symptomatic approach to the revolutionary process will focus on the nature of the uses to which new technologies are put and the way in which social forces affect those uses. Cliff Christians (1973, p. 224), for example, asks regarding home video technology: "Does cartridge (or cassette or disc) TV signify a revolution? Is this medium radically different in its fundamental nature?" In response to these questions, Christians implies that if video systems are implemented by the same economic and social forces as other media, the technology will not be revolutionary. A different "style" and a different "purpose" would signify for Christians a fundamentally different and revolutionary use that would "spawn a new communications era." The position is nothing much more than the Alternative Technologist's argument that the same technology utilized for different purposes is fundamentally revolutionary.

The revolutionary process from an expressive causal position places communication technologies well within—and sometimes at the heart of—the realm of an expressive totality. As might be expected, the definition of "communication" becomes more diffuse—like "technique"—and all aspects of society, including communication technologies, are depicted as aspects of communication. For example, James Carey (1969, pp. 23–24), taking a largely expressive position, writes:

In the 18th and 19th centuries western countries were hit with two successive waves of revolutions, revolutions separated in time but tied in logic. The first was the industrial revolution which reorganised the nature of work and the structural basis of class and community. The second was the revolution in communication and popular culture which reorganised the basis on which art, information, and culture was made available and the terms on which experience was worked into consciousness. While some commentators chose to treat these revolutions as independent events, it is obvious they stand as cause and effect, successive moments in the same process. The timing, interrelationship, speed, and extensiveness of these revolutions vary considerably from country to country, but both the direction of change and the major implications of these revolutions is everywhere the same.

Clearly, communication technologies here reflect some kind of essence; they are part and parcel of that essence that works itself out in society everywhere in much the same manner.

As these examples suggest, the communication revolution implies a relationship between communication technologies and society that is either mechanistic or expressive. In both positions, the communication revolution is indicative of fundamental change in all of society—fundamental, of course, as defined by the beholder. In a mechanistic position, the change is either caused by the technology or by the technology as shaped by social forces. In an expressive position, the change is part of a dualist relationship between center and periphery in which communication technologies or simply communications often constitute the essence of the homogeneous expressive totality. For both positions, societal change can be explained in terms of changes in communication and/or communication technologies. As Dudley Marcum (1978, p. 131) has stated, "Social or cultural revolutions are communications revolutions." Thus, to understand society, we need only begin by looking at its communication technologies and practices. A mechanistically oriented inquiry will look for the effects that the technologies brought or will bring about in order to determine whether they are revolutionary or evolutionary. The expressively oriented inquiry will look for correspondences between some essence of society and that of the technology to determine whether the essences are different enough to warrant the label "revolutionary."

The communication revolution thus embodies a tremendously technocentric or communicentric constitution of society. As such, communications and communication technologies are either primary causal determinants or essential expressions of a totality. The relationship between communication technologies and society is thus structurally a static one. Rather than addressing and analyzing the changing structural nature of the effective relationship between communication technologies and society, technologies and society are assumed to exist in similar structural relationships with regard to the effectivity of the technology. To look for social change as emanating from, or as expressed in, communication technologies and practices is to deny the historically constituted changing relationship between the complex social formation and communication technologies. We must understand the nature of that changing relationship if we are to correctly characterize the effective relationship between communication technologies and society and provide a basis for sound technological intervention.

The importance of critical analysis and intervention is particularly keen currently, with regard to what is often referred to as the "information age" or "information revolution." This age or revolution is so-called because it has been deemed that computers, fiber optics, satellites, and the like will reorganize our social order. Technology Assessment of the new technology, based on a mechanistic conception of the causal relationship between the technology and society, is likely to be concerned with mitigating possible disruption of the economic order caused by the new technologies. As was demonstrated in the previous chapter, finding ways to protect economic interests in software is a primary concern of the industry, its lawyers, and certain members of government. Those kinds of concerns, however, are expressed for far more than simply computer software. In an article titled "How to Sell Nothing and Get Rich," a representative of Bell Northern Research in Ottawa implies that a major concern regarding technologies such as videotex and teletext is assuring that the economic patterns of profiting from communication technologies be preserved. He writes:

A clear understanding of how wealth is created in an information society is clearly essential and if, as it is my belief, it is found to be through the social process of information evaluation, then our perception of the role of network must be very much enlarged, for now it becomes the mainstay of tomorrow's economic engine (Thompson, 1980, p. 15).

While Technology Assessment will intervene in the relationship between technologies and society in order to streamline implementation within the social order, Alternative Technologists whose analyses are based on symptomatic causality will be busily attempting to "liberate" the new technologies for their own use, oblivious to their contribution to the health of just that which they profess to despise. In an article titled "Toward Convivial Computing," Terry Winograd (1980) discusses ways in which computers can be made to be more convivial, that is, that programs can be "designed to work with the natural modes of human thought and communication, rather than demanding a 'computerized attitude' on the part of those who interact with them" (p. 59). While such a development might please many an Alternative Technologist and has in fact occurred in response to the kind of complaints launched by the Alternative Technology movement, the uses to which these programs may be put are not limited to the "liberated," "revolutionary" uses of an Alternative Technology movement. Furthermore, the convivial programs might well make it possible for software interests to expand their markets for computer software and hardware to otherwise reticent sectors of society.

Other Alternative Technologists and Luddites whose analyses are based on simple causal positions, can only call for the abolition of the technologies they object to because the technology is inherently at fault.

Finally, the pessimists, the intellectual Luddites who base their analyses in expressive causal terms, will search for correspondences between the social order and the information technologies. Typically, the computer becomes the essence or metaphor of the age; we give ourselves over to it and are engulfed in the logic of its unfolding.

Yet what of intervention? The uncritical maintenance of the eco-

nomic status quo . . . the unexamined contribution to its health . . . calling for abolition of technologies of social structures without a carefully
worked out critical analysis as support . . . or the intellectual paralysis of
researchers trapped by their own faulty logic—these are inadequate,
feeble excuses for effective intervention. By basing analysis and intervention on a conception of the structural causal relationship between
communication technologies and society, however, truly informed intervention is possible.

Critical analysis of the information age must begin with a rejection
of the very premises on which the issue is initially raised. There is no
information age or revolution—no fundamentally different technologies that will either cause a new social order or reflect the essence of a
new social totality. Analysis must begin without a technocentric or communicentric image of society. Rather, the new technologies are a part of
a complex social formation, and we must explore the particular historically specific effective relationships between those technologies and the
social formation in order to critically evaluate those relationships and
propose strategies for intervention. The case study conducted in the
previous chapter on the changing effective relationship between patent
law and the invention and innovation of communication technologies
represents a step in the direction toward a comprehensive understanding of the dominant effective relationships among the levels of the complex structured whole and communication technologies. The analysis
not only contributes to an understanding of the shifts in the effective
aspects of those relationships, but it also points to some particularly
significant, though frighteningly unchallenged, contemporary developments in those relationships. Specifically, contemporary communication
industries, acting within the ideology of the right to own property—
intellectual and real—are developing technologies that they seek to protect such that our very means of communication and our communication
practices will be still further subjugated to capitalist relations of production. By developing and defining computer programs so that they look
like traditionally protected intellectual property as defined in patent,
copyright, or trade secret law, what our media look like and how we
communicate will be altered. Alternatively, by changing patent,
copyright, or trade secret law to extend protection to computer programs, the nature of the capitalist control of property will undergo a
change. Although we must critically evaluate these processes, the issue is
far greater than that of computer software alone. We must challenge the
facts that communication technologies are invented and innovated to
generate surplus profit, that they are protected as property, and that
they thereby enhance monopoly capital's control over labor, the means
of communication, and communication practices.

The consequences, some of which were discussed in more detail in the previous chapter, seem to demand intervention. Yet we must know how and where to intervene effectively. In the previous chapter, the suggestion was that intervention occur at the site of the attempts to extend patent protection to computer programs. The analysis conducted in that chapter, however, was only a first step, and additional work can only enhance understanding and improve prescriptions for effective intervention. In particular, other means of protecting intellectual property require a thorough critique, specifically copyright law and trade secret law. The origins of the ideology of progress and its effective relationship in the social formation might likewise be revealing, as might an analysis of political regulatory practices such as antitrust law. Most important, however, is the need for a careful analysis of the role of elites in the social formation. The compelling need to understand the role of elites is illustrated by a major weakness of the analysis of patent law in this book. Although the proposal is to intervene at the site of attempts to extend patent protection to computer programs, the success of such an intervention cannot be guaranteed. One reason is that this book's analysis lacks an adequate theory of political power and of the nature of the politically effective relationships between the various fractions of the capitalist class. Without such an analysis, the resulting inadequate understanding of the changing alliances between monopoly capital and government is likely to hinder effective implementation of the generalized strategy for intervention. By building our understanding of the complex relationships between the economic, political, and ideological conditions of existence, we can hope to liberate the development of communication technologies and practices from the logic of capitalist domination.

Bibliography

Althusser, L. (1970). *For Marx*. B. Brewster (Trans.). New York: Random House, Vintage Books.

Althusser, L. (1971). *Lenin and Philosophy and Other Essays*. B. Brewster (Trans.). New York: Monthly Review Press.

Althusser, L. (1976). *Essays in Self-Criticism*. G. Lock (Trans.). London: New Left Books.

Althusser, L., and Balibar, E. (1977). *Reading Capital*. B. Brewster (Trans.). London: New Left Books.

Aronson, S. H. (1977). "Bell's Electrical Toy: What's the Use? The Sociology of Early Telephone Usage." In I. de Sola Pool (Ed.), *The Social Impact of the Telephone*. MIT Bicentennial Studies, Vol. 1. Cambridge: MIT Press.

Athanasiou, T. (1979). "Stafford Beer: The Untechnocrat and His Liberty Machine: A Review of the CYBERSYN Project." *The Journal of Community Communications 3* (No. 2), 6–16.

Berg, M. R. (1981). "The Politics of Technology Assessment." In T. J. Kuehn and A. L. Porter (Eds.), *Science, Technology, and National Policy*. Ithaca: Cornell University Press. Originally published in *Journal of International Society for Technology Assessment* 1 (December), 1975.

Berry, J. (1970). *The Luddites in Yorkshire*. Clapham, England: Dalesman Publishing Co.

Billington, D. P. (1974). "Structures and Machines: The Two Sides of Technology." *Soundings 57* (No. 3), 275–288.

Bittner, J. R. (1980). *Mass Communication: An Introduction*, 2d ed. Englewood Cliffs, N.J.: Prentice-Hall, Inc.

Bohm, D. (1980). *Causality and Chance in Modern Physics*. Philadelphia: University of Pennsylvania Press.

Boroush, M., Chen, K., and Christakis, A. (1980). *Technology Assessment: Creative Futures*. New York: North Holland.

149

Brand, M. (Ed.). (1976). *The Nature of Causation*. Urbana: University of Illinois Press.

Braverman, H. (1974). *Labor and Monopoly Capital: The Degradation of Work in the Twentieth Century*. New York: Monthly Review Press.

Brooks, H. (1979). "Technology Assessment in Retrospect." In J. G. Burke and M. C. Eakin (Eds.). *Technology and Change*. San Francisco: Boyd & Fraser Publishing Co. Originally published in *Newsletter on Science, Technology and Human Values* (Harvard University) 17 (October), 1976.

Brooks, J. (1975). *Telephone: The First Hundred Years*. New York: Harper & Row.

Brown, H. F. (1891). *The Venetian Printing Press: An Historical Study Based upon Documents for the Most Part Hitherto Unpublished*. London: John C. Nimmo.

Bunge, M. (1979). *Causality and Modern Science*, 3d ed. New York: Dover Publications.

Butler, P. (1940). *The Origin of Printing in Europe*. Chicago: The University of Chicago Press.

Carey, J. W. (1969). "The Communications Revolution and the Professional Communicator." *The Sociological Review Monograph 13* (January), 23–38.

Carey, J. W., and Quirk, J. J. (1970). "The Mythos of the Electronic Revolution." Part I: *The American Scholar 39* (Autumn), 219–241; Part II: *The American Scholar 39* (Summer), 395–424.

Cavanagh, M. (1977). "Write On." *Peace News for Nonviolent Revolution 2047* (July 1), 15.

Cherry, C. (1977). "The Telephone System: Creator of Mobility and Social Change." In I. de Sola Pool (Ed.), *The Social Impact of the Telephone*. MIT Bicentennial Studies, Vol. 1. Cambridge: MIT Press.

Christians, C. (1973). "Home Video Systems. A Revolution?" *Journal of Broadcasting 17* (Spring), 223–234.

Coates, J. (1974). "The Identification and Selection of Candidates and Priorities for Technology Assessment." *Technology Assessment 2* (No. 2), 77–104.

Coon, H. (1939). *American Tel & Tel: The Story of a Great Monopoly*. New York: Longmans, Green and Co.

Daddario, E. Q. (1968). "Technology Assessment—A Legislative View." *George Washington Law Review 36*, 1044–1059.

Danielian, N. R. (1939). *A.T.&T.: The Story of Industrial Conquest*. New York: The Vanguard Press.

Dann, Commissioner of Patents and Trademarks v. Johnston. 425 US 219 (1976).

Descartes, R. (1637). "Discourse on the Method of Rightly Conducting the Reason and Seeking Truth in the Field of Science." Reprinted in L. J. Lafleur (Trans.) (1960), *Discourse on Method and Meditations*. New York: Bobbs-Merrill Co., The Library of Liberal Arts.

Dickson, D. (1974). *Alternative Technology and the Politics of Technical Change*. Glasgow: William Collins Sons & Co., Fontana.

Dickson, E. M. with Bowers, R. (1974). *The Video Telephone: Impact of a New Era in Telecommunications*. New York: Praeger Publishers.

Eagleton, T. (1978). *Criticism and Ideology*. London: New Left Books, Verso.

Elliot, D. (1979). "No Fixed Shopping List." *Peace News for Nonviolent Revolution 2105* (September 12), 12–13.

Ellul, J. (1964). *The Technological Society*. New York: Random House, Vintage.

Ellul, J. (1973). *Propaganda: The Formation of Men's Attitudes*. New York: Random House, Vintage. (Originally published, 1965).

Emerson, S. (1979). "Warning: Technology Issue/Issues in Technology." *The Journal of Community Communications 3* (No. 2), 1–2.

Everson, G. (1949). *The Story of Television: The Life of Philo T. Farnsworth*. New York: W. W. Norton & Co.

Federico, P. J. (1929a). "Colonial Monopolies and Patents." *Journal of the Patent Office Society 11* (No. 8), 358–365.

Federico, P. J. (1929b). "Origin and Early History of Patents." *Journal of the Patent Office Society 11* (No. 7), 292–305.

Federico, P. J. (1932). "The First Patent Act." *Journal of the Patent Office Society 14* (No. 4), 237–252.

Fenning, K. (1929). "The Origin of the Patent and Copyright Clause of the Constitution." *Journal of the Patent Office Society 11* (March), 438–445. Originally published in *Georgetown Law Journal* 17 (February), 1929, 109–117.

Folk, G. E. (1942). *Patents and Industrial Progress: A Summary, Analysis, and Evaluation of the Record on Patents of the Temporary National Economic Committee.* New York: Harper & Brothers Publishers.

Fuhrmann, O. W. (1938). "The Invention of Printing." In L. C. Wroth (Ed.), *A History of the Printed Book.* New York: The Limited Editions Club.

Gates, A. (1977). "From the Luddites." *Peace News for Nonviolent Revolution 2044* (May 20), 14.

Geduld, H. M. (1975). *The Birth of the Talkies: From Edison to Jolson.* Bloomington: Indiana University Press.

Giddens, A. (1979). *Central Problems in Social Theory: Action, Structure and Contradiction in Social Analysis.* Berkeley: University of California Press.

Goetz, M. A. (1978). "The 'What Is Software?' Legal Snafu." *ICP Interface: Data Processing Management 3* (No. 3), 22, 24–25.

Goetz, M. A. (1979). "Software Packages: Best Buy Today." *Datamation 25* (No. 14), 136–137.

Gottschalk, Acting Commissioner of Patents v. Benson et al. 409 US 63 (1972).

Hall, S. (1980). "Cultural Studies: Two Paradigms." *Media, Culture and Society 2,* 57–72.

Hamilton, A., Madison, J., and Jay, J. (1852). *The Federalist,* new ed. Hallowell: Masters, Smith & Co.

Hegel, G. W. F. (1967). *The Phenomenology of Mind.* J. B. Baillie (Trans.). Introduction by G. Lichtheim. New York: Harper & Row, Harper Torchbooks, The Academy Library.

Hendricks, G. (1961). *The Edison Motion Picture Myth.* Berkeley: University of California Press.

Hershey, C. and Sachter, E. (1976). "Acquiring Baseline Data on Potential Uses of New Communication Technologies." *Journal of the International Society for Technology Assessment 2* (No. 2), 51–61.

Hobsbawm, E. J. (1952). "The Machine Breakers." *Past and Present 1* (February), 57–70.

Horkheimer, M. (1972). *Critical Theory: Selected Essays.* M. J. O'Connell et al. (Trans.). New York: Seabury Press.

Houlton, R. (1973). "Innovation, Intervention and Media Analysis: An Examination of the Pattern of Change in the U.S. Mass Entertainment Industry with Special Reference to the Post-1940 Period." Unpublished dissertation, University of Leeds.

Hume, D. (1955). *An Inquiry Concerning Human Understanding.* C. W. Hendell (Ed.). New York: Bobbs-Merrill Co., The Liberal Arts Press. Reprinted in part in M. Brand (Ed.) (1976), *The Nature of Causation.* Urbana: University of Illinois Press.

Illich, I. (1973). *Tools for Conviviality.* New York: Harper & Row, Perennial.

The Journal of Community Communications (1979). *3* (No. 2).

Kahn, A. E. (1940). "Fundamental Deficiencies of the American Patent Law." *The American Economic Review 30* (No. 3), 475–491.

Keet, E. E. (1979). "ICP Interview: Lee Keet." *ICP Interface: Data Processing Management 4* (No. 1), 8–11.

Kern, C. (1981). "Washington Tackles the Software Problem." *Byte 6* (No. 5), 128–138.
Kingsbury, J. E. (1915). *The Telephone and Telephone Exchanges: Their Invention and Development.* London: Longmans, Green, and Co.
Klein, S. (1979). "The Home Information Appliance: An Introduction to Prestel." *The Journal of Community Communications 3* (No. 2), 17–18.
Klitzke, R. A. (1959). "Historical Background of the English Patent Law." *Journal of the Patent Office Society 41* (September), 615–650.
Kurtz, R. E. (1978). "Survey of the Law on Software as Applied to Patents." In G. B. Coplein and A. E. Hirsch, Jr., *Current Developments in Patent Law: 1978.* New York: Practising Law Institute.
Lenin, V. (1917). *State and Revolution.* Reprinted in A. E. Mendel (Ed.) (1961), *Essential Works of Marxism.* New York: National General, Bantam, 1961.
Lessing, L. (1956). *Man of High Fidelity: Edwin Howard Armstrong.* New York: J. B. Lippincott Co.
Lowe, A. M. (1979a). "Patenting of Computer Programs (Firmware and Software)." Paper presented at the American Federation of Information Processing Societies National Computer Conference (June). Mimeographed.
Lowe, A. M. (ca. 1979b). "Report of the ABA Subcommittee on Recent Computer Programming Cases." Mimeographed.
Lukács, G. (1966). "Technology and Social Relations." *New Left Review* 39 (September/October), 27–34.
Lukács, G. (1972). *History and Class Consciousness: Studies in Marxist Dialectics.* R. Livingstone (Trans.). Cambridge: MIT Press.
Lukács, G. (1976). *The Young Hegel: Studies in the Relations between Dialectics and Economics.* R. Livingstone (Trans.). Cambridge: MIT Press.
Maclaurin, W. (1971). *Invention and Innovation in the Radio Industry.* Massachusetts Institute of Technology Studies of Innovation. Reprint. New York: Arno Press and The New York Times.
Mandich, G. (1948). "Venetian Patents (1450–1550)." *Journal of the Patent Office Society 30* (No. 3), 166–241.
Marcum, D. (1978). "Computer Revolutions: Reflections on New Communications Technologies and Revolutionary Change in Systems." Unpublished dissertation, University of Illinois.
Marcuse, H. (1941). "Some Social Implications of Modern Technology." *Studies in Philosophy and Social Science 9,* 414–439.
Marcuse, H. (1964). *One-Dimensional Man: Studies in the Ideology of Advanced Industrial Society.* Boston: Beacon Press.
Marx, K. (1972). Preface to *A Contribution to the Critique of Political Economy.* In R. C. Tucker (Ed.), *The Marx-Engels Reader.* New York: W. W. Norton & Co.
Marx, K., and Engels, F. (1970). *The German Ideology.* Part one, with selections from parts two and three and supplementary texts. C. J. Arthur (Ed.). New York: International Publishers.
McLuhan, M., and Fiore, Q. (1967). *The Medium Is the Massage: An Inventory of Effects.* New York: Bantam Books.
Mendel, A. P. (Ed.). (1961). *Essential Works of Marxism.* New York: National General, Bantam.
Mitcham, C. and Mackey, R. (Eds.). (1972). *Philosophy and Technology: Readings in the Philosophical Problems of Technology.* New York: The Macmillan Co., The Free Press.
Moodies Public Utilities Manual 1980, Vol. 1. (1980). New York: Dunn and Bradstreet.
Moyer, J. A. (1977). "Urban Growth and the Development of the Telephone: Some Relationships at the Turn of the Century." In I. de Sola Pool (Ed.), *The Social Impact of the Telephone.* MIT Bicentennial Studies, Vol. 1. Cambridge: MIT Press.

Mumford, L. (1963). *Technics and Civilization*. New York: Harcourt, Brace & World, Harbinger.

Mumford, L. (1967). *Technics and Human Development. The Myth of the Machine*, Vol. 1. New York: Harcourt Brace Jovanovich, Harvest.

Mumford, L. (1970). *The Pentagon of Power. The Myth of the Machine*, Vol. 2. New York: Harcourt Brace Jovanovich, Harvest.

Myers, E. D. (1978). "Should Software Be Copyrighted?" *Datamation 24* (No. 3), 125.

Myers, E. D. (1979a). "Of Bells and Horses." *Datamation 25* (No. 14), 51–53.

Myers, E. D. (1979b). "What Is Software?" *Datamation 25* (No. 3), 74–75.

Nelson, T. (1977). *The Home Computer Revolution*. South Bend: Theodor H. Nelson.

Noble, D. F. (1979). *America by Design: Science, Technology, and the Rise of Corporate Capitalism*. Oxford: Oxford University Press.

Nycum, S. H. (1978). "Legal Protection for Computer Programs." *Computer Law Journal 1* (No. 1), 1–83.

Oppenheim, S. C. (1951). "A New Approach to Evaluation of the American Patent System." *Journal of the Patent Office Society 33* (No. 8), 555–568.

Pagenberg, B. A. (1974). "Patentability of Computer Programs on the National and International Level." *International Review of Industrial Property and Copyright Law 5*, 1–43.

Parker, Acting Commissioner of Patents and Trademarks v. Flook. US, 57 L Ed 2nd 451 (1978).

Parker, E. B. (1976). "Social Implications of Computer/Telecoms Systems." *Telecommunications Policy 1* (December), 3–20.

Parker, E. B., with the assistance of Porat, M. (1976). "Background Report." *OECD Informatics Studies No. 11: Conference on Computer/Telecommunications Policy*, Proceedings of the OECD Conference (February 4–6). (1975). Paris: OECD.

Perrin, N. (1980). *Giving Up the Gun: Japan's Reversion to the Sword, 1543–1879*. Boulder: Shambhala.

Pfeifer, M. R., Esq. (1978). "Legal Protection of Computer Software: An Update." *Orange County Bar Journal 5* (Fall), 226–247.

Pierce, J. R. (1977). "The Telephone and Society in the Past 100 Years." In I. de Sola Pool (Ed.), *The Social Impact of the Telephone*. MIT Bicentennial Studies, Vol. 1. Cambridge: MIT Press.

Pool, I. de Sola (Ed.). (1977). *The Social Impact of the Telephone*. MIT Bicentennial Studies, Vol. 1. Cambridge: MIT Press.

Popper, H. R. (1977). "Technology and Programming—Is It a Problem in Definitions?" *APLA Quarterly Journal, 5* 13–29.

Porter, A. L. et al. (1980). *A Guidebook for Technology Assessment Analysis*. New York: North Holland.

Poulantzas, N. (1978a). *Classes in Contemporary Capitalism*. D. Fernbach (Trans.). London: New Left Books, Verso.

Poulantzas, N. (1978b). *Political Power and Social Classes*. T. O'Hagan (Trans.). London: New Left Books, Verso.

Prager, F. D. (1944). "A History of Intellectual Property from 1545–1787." *Journal of the Patent Office Society 26* (No. 11), 711–760.

Prager, F. D. (1952). "The Early Growth and Influence of Intellectual Property." *Journal of the Patent Office Society 34* (No. 2), 106–140.

Prindle, E. J. (1906). "Patents as a Factor in a Manufacturing Business: I. Their Influence in Making Markets and Commanding Success." *The Engineering Magazine 31* (No. 6), 809–816.

Putnam, L. H., and Fitzsimmons, A. (1979). "Estimating Software Costs." *Datamation 25* (No. 12), 137–138, 140.

Reece, R. (1979). *The Sun Betrayed: A Report on the Corporate Seizure of U.S. Solar Energy Development*. Boston: South End Press.

Roszak, T. (1978). *Person/Planet: The Creative Disintegration of Industrial Society.* Garden City: Anchor Press, Doubleday.

Schiller, H. I. (1978). "Computer Systems: Power for Whom and for What?" *Journal of Communication 28* (No. 4), 184–193.

Schmookler, J. (1972). *Patents, Invention, and Economic Change: Data and Selected Essays.* Z. Griliches and L. Hurwicz (Eds.). Cambridge: Harvard University Press.

Slack, J. D. (1981). "Programming Protection: The Problem of Software." *Journal of Communication 31* (No. 1), 151–163.

Slack, J. D. (forthcoming). "Surveying the Impacts of Communication Technologies." In B. Dervin and M. Voigt (Eds.). *Progress in Communication Sciences 5.* Norwood, N.J.: Ablex.

Smith, R. L. (1972). *The Wired Nation: Cable TV: The Electronic Communications Highway.* New York: Harper & Row.

Solomon, R. J. (1978). "What Happened after Bell Spilled the Acid? Telecommunications History: A View through the Literature." *Telecommunications Policy 2* (June), 146–157.

Sutter, W. (1976). "Background Report." *OECD Informatics Studies No. 11: Conference on Computer/Telecommunications Policy,* Proceedings of the OECD Conference (February 4–6). (1975). Paris: OECD.

Taylor, C. (1975). *Hegel.* Cambridge, England: Cambridge University Press.

Taylor, R. (1967). "Causation." *The Encyclopedia of Philosophy 2,* 56–66.

Teich, A. H. (Ed.). (1977). *Technology and Man's Future,* 2d ed. New York: St. Martin's Press.

Thomis, M. I. (1972). *The Luddites: Machine-Breaking in Regency England.* New York: Schocken Books.

Thompson, E. P. (1963). *The Making of the English Working Class.* New York: Random House, Vintage Books.

Thompson, G. B. (1980). "How to Sell Nothing and Get Rich." *Intermedia 8* (No. 6), 14–15.

Thompson, R. L. (1947). *Wiring a Continent: The History of the Telegraph Industry in the United States 1832–1866.* Princeton: Princeton University Press.

Tykociner Files. University of Illinois Archives. Urbana, Ill.

U.S. Congress, House of Representatives. (1967). 90th Cong., 1st sess., H.R. 6698, 1967. Washington, D.C.: Government Printing Office.

U.S. Congress, House of Representatives. (1969a). Committee on Science and Astronautics. *A Study of Technology Assessment.* Report of the Committee on Public Engineering Policy of the National Academy of Engineering. 91st Cong., 1st sess. Washington, D.C.: Government Printing Office.

U.S. Congress, House of Representatives. (1969b). Committee on Science and Astronautics. *Technology: Processes of Assessment and Choice.* Report of the National Academy of Sciences. 91st Cong., 1st sess. Washington, D.C.: Government Printing Office.

U.S. Congress, Senate. Committee on the Judiciary. (1958a). Subcommittee on Patents, Trademarks, and Copyrights. *Economic Aspects of Patents and the American Patent System: A Bibliography.* 85th Cong., 2d sess. Washington, D.C.: Government Printing Office.

U.S. Congress, Senate. (1958b). Committee on the Judiciary. Subcommittee on Patents, Trademarks, and Copyrights. *An Economic Review of the Patent System,* by Fritz Machlup. 85th Cong., 2d sess. Committee Print, Study No. 15. Washington, D.C.: Government Printing Office.

U.S. Congress. (1975). Office of Technology Assessment. *Annual Report to the Congress for 1974/1975.* Washington, D.C.: Government Printing Office.

U.S. Congress, (1976). Office of Technology Assessment. *The Feasibility and Value of Broadband Communications in Rural Areas: A Preliminary Evaluation.* Staff Report (April). Washington, D.C.: Government Printing Office.

U.S. Congress. (1979). Office of Technology Assessment. *Annual Report to the Congress for 1978.* Washington, D.C.: Government Printing Office.

U.S. Congress. (1981). Office of Technology Assessment. *Computer-Based National Information Systems.* Washington, D.C.: Office of Technology Assessment.

U.S. Department of Commerce, National Bureau of Standards. (1977). *Copyright in Computer Readable Works: Policy Impacts of Technological Change,* by Roy G. Saltman, NBS Special Publication No. 500–17. Washington, D.C.: Government Printing Office.

U.S. Federal Communications Commission. (1939). *Investigation of the Telephone Industry in the United States.* 76th Cong., 1st sess. Washington, D.C.: Government Printing Office.

U.S. President's Commission on the Patent System. (1966). *Report* (November 17). Washington, D.C.: Government Printing Office.

United States Patent Law of 1952 as Amended 35 U.S.C.A.

Vaitsos, C. (1972). "Patents Revisited: Their Function in Developing Countries." *The Journal of Development Studies 9* (No. 1), 71–97.

Vaughan, F. L. (1956). *The United States Patent System: Legal and Economic Conflicts in American Patent History.* Norman: University of Oklahoma Press.

Wallis, J. (1977). "Computers in the Alternative Society." *Peace News for Nonviolent Revolution 2043* (May 6), 8.

Williams, R. (1965). *The Long Revolution.* Middlesex: Penguin Books.

Williams, R. (1973). "Base and Superstructure in Marxist Cultural Theory." *New Left Review 82* (November/December), 3–16.

Williams, R. (1975). *Television: Technology and Cultural Form.* New York: Schocken Books.

Williams, R. (1976). *Keywords: A Vocabulary of Culture and Society.* New York: Oxford University Press.

Williams, R. (1977). *Marxism and Literature.* Oxford: Oxford University Press.

Williams, R. (1979). *Politics and Letters: Interviews with New Left Review.* London: New Left Books.

Winner, L. (1977a). *Autonomous Technology: Technics-out-of-Control as a Theme in Political Thought.* Cambridge: MIT Press.

Winner, L. (1977b). "On Criticizing Technology." In A. H. Teich, *Technology and Man's Future.* New York: St. Martin's Press. Originally published in *Public Policy* 20 (No. 1), 1972, 35–59.

Winograd, T. (1980). "Toward Convivial Computing." In M. L. Dertouzos and J. Moses (Eds.). *The Computer Age: A Twenty-Year View.* MIT Bicentennial Studies, Vol. 6. Cambridge: MIT Press.

World Peace through Law Center, Section on Law and Computer Technology. "Model Provisions on the Protection of Computer Software." *Law and Computer Technology 11* (No. 1), 2–27.

Author Index

Subject Index